Melville J. Herskovits

Leaders of Modern Anthropology Series
Charles Wagley, GENERAL EDITOR

MELVILLE J. HERSKOVITS

by George Eaton Simpson

Columbia University Press

1973 NEW YORK AND LONDON

301.2
Si 5m
92194
Feb. 1975

Library of Congress Cataloging in Publication Data

Simpson, George Eaton, 1904–
Melville J. Herskovits.

(Leaders of modern anthropology series)
"Selections from the writings of Melville J.
Herskovits": p. 105
Bibliography: p. 189
1. Herskovits, Melville Jean, 1895–1963.
2. Ethnology—Africa, West—Addresses, essays,
lectures. I. Herskovits, Melville Jean, 1895–1963.
II. Series.
GN21.H47S55   301.2′092′4 [B]   73–5966
ISBN 0-231-03385-0
ISBN 0-231-03396-6 (pbk.)

Preface

✛ I spent a memorable semester working with Melville Herskovits as a Social Science Research Council postdoctoral fellow in 1936, and during the summer session of 1956 I taught courses in anthropology at Northwestern University, where he was a professor. I knew him as a friend for thirty years and as a colleague in African and Afroamerican studies for the same length of time.

I hope that the biographical sketch, my view of the nature of his work, and the selections from some of his writings that follow will convey some idea of Melville Herskovits' personality, his contributions to the science of anthropology, and of the time in which he lived and worked. I hope also that some of the readers of this volume will continue their reading in Herskovits' own works. In her introduction to *The New World Negro: Selected Papers in Afroamerican Studies*, which she also edited, Frances S. Herskovits presents an interesting commentary on her husband's view of Afroamerican studies. She also writes about the influence of his field experiences in Africa and in the New World on his thinking and his career.

I am deeply grateful to Peter B. Hammond for reading the text and making extremely useful comments and suggestions. For information about Melville Herskovits as a person contained in published materials (articles, obituaries, and memorial tributes) and personal communications, I am indebted to his sister, Mrs. Samuel Levy; his daughter, Jean Herskovits; and to Margaret Mead, William R. Bascom, Francis L. K. Hsu, Joseph H. Greenberg, Alan P. Merriam, Peter B. Hammond, James W. Fernandez, Gwendolyn Carter, Jacques Maquet, and the University Relations Department of Northwestern University. Charles Wagley, editor of the Leaders of Modern Anthropology Series, and John D. Moore of Columbia University Press have given valuable advice and help. Photographs of Herskovits were kindly provided by the National Academy of Sciences, the Program of African Studies, and the University Relations Department of Northwestern University. The staff of the stenographic office of Oberlin College was most helpful in preparing the manuscript for publication.

I am grateful to the following for permission to reprint materials in this book: *American Magazine of Art,* J. J. Augustin, Columbia University Press, *Journal of Negro History, Bijdragen Tot de Taal-, Land- en Volkenkunde,* Bobbs-Merrill, Harper & Row, *Institut Français d'Afrique Noire,* Alfred A. Knopf, Inc., *Southwestern Journal of Anthropology,* and the University of Chicago Press.

GEORGE E. SIMPSON

Contents

Contents

Melville J. Herskovits

PART I

Herskovits' Life and Work

I INTRODUCTION: HERSKOVITS AS SCIENTIST AND AS MAN

It is surprising that Melville J. Herskovits, the founder of scientific Afroamerican studies and the first Africanist in the United States, has not been more widely recognized as the foremost and the most sophisticated of the early leaders in the Afroamerican field, a group that included Fernando Ortiz in Cuba, Jean Price-Mars in Haiti, and Artur Ramos in Brazil. An examination of Herskovits' life work reveals clearly the importance in today's world of his research and his thinking about African cultures and the various combinations of these and European cultures in the New World.

Melville Jean Herskovits was born in Bellefontaine, Ohio, on September 10, 1895, and died in Evanston, Illinois, on February 25, 1963. His father, Herman, a clothing merchant, was born in Hungary. His mother, Henrietta Hart Herskovits, was born in Germany. Because of his mother's being ill, his family moved to El Paso, Texas, when Herskovits was ten years old. Little is known about the several years he spent in Texas; one former student, however, recalls that Herskovits talked knowledgeably to him about the cowboys' way of life. After his mother's death, the family moved to Erie, Pennsylvania, where Herskovits graduated from high school in 1912. Other than academic studies, Herskovits' principal interest during his youth was music, especially playing the violin. In 1915 he enrolled at the University of Cincinnati, and, for theological studies, at the Hebrew Union College. After Medical-Corps service in World War I, Herskovits entered the University of Chicago. He graduated as a major in history in 1920. One of his undergraduate interests was biology, a subject related to his later interest in physical anthropology. At the time of Herskovits' studies at Chicago, anthropology had not become known as an undergraduate area of specialization. According to Joseph H. Greenberg, "like many others who became professionals, he first became seriously interested in anthropology as a career in the course of his graduate studies. It was then that he came under the influence of Alexander A. Goldenweiser of the New School for Social Research and of Franz Boas at Columbia University in New York.

In anthropology as conceived by these men, Herskovits found the methodology for the study of human history and behavior and a body of theoretical knowledge which supplied what he felt was lacking in other disciplines in which he had worked . . ." (Greenberg, 1971, 66). Thorstein Veblen was another influence in Herskovits' intellectual development. Herskovits knew him both at the New School and later in Washington. He took his A.M. and Ph.D. degrees in anthropology at Columbia University in 1921 and 1923. Frequently Herskovits tried to keep up the spirits of his own graduate students by regaling them with stories of the many odd jobs he had held in New York during his postgraduate study. At one time, for example, he worked as a shoe clerk at Macy's. At another time he served as a spear-carrying extra in a performance of *Aida*.

Margaret Mead has kindly written the following recollections about the graduate students in anthropology at Columbia in the early 1920s.

> *Mel Herskovits was a graduate student at Columbia when I was a senior at Barnard and had already begun attending all of Boas' courses. He came from the New School for Social Research where he encountered Elsie Clews Parsons and knew Ruth Bene-*

dict. He finished his work for his degree (we didn't get them in those days until the thesis was published) in 1923, the year I formally entered the department. He and Frances had an attractive and bohemian apartment near Columbia. The year before his marriage he lived near the old New School, in the Chelsea District, and had a cat named Jezebel to whom he fed liver most extravagantly. There were not enough of us for rivalries; those were lean years when Boas' department was being starved by Columbia. In all, we were Irving Hallowell, who came over from Philadelphia, Ruth Benedict, who finished in 1922 but continued to work within the Department of Folklore, Isabel Gordon Carter, and a man whose sister later married Goldenweiser. During my two years, Mel used to come to seminars and to lunch, which the whole department held every week. I had several ties to him—his room-mate was Malcolm Willey, the sociologist, who at that time was engaged to Nancy Body, who lived in the same apartment as I did. I was also a close friend of the psychologist, Ethel Goldsmith Muegel, who was from Cincinnati, and had known Mel when he was a student at Hebrew Union. So he used to come to our parties. He came to my wedding in 1923, when, I remember, he had just heard that he had got the NRC Fellowship.

Mel was a bouncing, cheerful, unsquelchable extrovert, writing with gusto, and a fair pride in what he produced. One of his famous remarks—when we had all gone to dinner in Chinatown—was 'I don't expect to be a Boas, but I do expect to be a Lowie or an Ogburn,' a remark at that point not appreciated by Dorothy Thomas who admired Ogburn very much. (Personal communication from Margaret Mead, April 12, 1973.)

Herskovits and Frances S. Shapiro were married in 1924, and their daughter, Jean Frances, now an associate professor of African history at the State University of New York, College at Purchase, was born in 1935. Mrs. Herskovits died on May 4, 1972, in Evanston, Illinois.

As a Fellow in anthropology of the Board of Biological Science, National Research Council, from 1923 until 1926, Herskovits pursued studies in physical anthropology entitled "Variability under Radical Crossing." During the years 1924–1927, he lectured at Columbia

Melville J. Herskovits

University, and in 1925 he was assistant professor of anthropology at Howard University. His teaching at Howard led to a number of friendships with members of the Howard faculty which continued over a long period of years. Among the Howard colleagues of that and later years with whom he carried on spirited and fruitful dialogues were Alain Locke, E. Franklin Frazier, Ralph Bunche, Abram Harris, Sterling Brown, and Charles H. Thompson.

He began his long career at Northwestern University in 1927, serving in turn as assistant, associate, and full professor of anthropology. In 1961 he was appointed there to the first Chair of African Studies in the United States. In many ways the situation was rather trying for the Herskovitses during the early years at Northwestern. At that time, there was considerable anti-Semitism at the university. Moreover, Herskovits, the university's only anthropologist, was a member of the department of sociology. Also, it was difficult to obtain funds at a conservative institution to study Africans and Afroamericans. Herskovits persisted nevertheless, and the Northwestern Department of Anthropology and the University Interdisciplinary Program of African Studies were created largely by the strength of his personal drive.

The honors and distinctions that Melville Herskovits received and the professional services that he performed were numerous. In 1937–1938, he was a Guggenheim Memorial Fellow. During World War II he served on the Board of Economic Warfare as Chief Consultant for African Affairs. In 1950, he was editor of the *International Directory of Anthropologists*, and he edited the *American Anthropologist* during the years 1949–1952. He was president of the American Folklore Society (1945) and of the African Studies Association (1957–1958). He was a Viking Fund Medalist in 1953, a member of the National Academy of Sciences, and a recipient of decorations from the governments of Haiti and of the Netherlands. At Northwestern he was a moving spirit in the development of an interdisciplinary course in anthropology, psychology, and sociology. He served on many committees, often as chairman, appointed by the American Anthropological Association, the American Council of Learned Societies, and the Social Science Research Council. In 1934 he held the office of Vice President of the American Association for the Advancement of Science; in 1947 he was a member of the executive board of the American Anthropological Association, and he was chosen as a member of the Permanent Council of the International Anthropology Congress. In December 1962, Herskovits played a major role in the organization of the First International Congress of Africanists, a meeting held in Ghana. In 1970, Northwestern University named its Africana library collection, one of the largest in the United States, for him.

Herskovits was not an easy taskmaster. Over the years, the admired and the resented aspects of his character were the subject of endless fascination and continuous speculation among Northwestern's graduate students in anthropology. Often, there seemed to be as much talk about Mel as about anthropology. Speaking for all of Herskovits' students at the memorial service held on March 2, 1963, Alan P. Merriam said: "He drove us on, he pushed and prodded, and it was sometimes exasperating. Whose ears among us have not burned at one time or another when we heard, in no uncertain terms, that he was not yet satisfied? But he knew when to stop and when to praise, and we learned, finally, not to cringe when the paper came back blackened, because we said, the blacker it is the better he thinks it is and the more willing, therefore, to give it his time and energy" (Merriam, 1963).

Herskovits loved intellectual exchanges in the seminar, at the luncheon table, at conferences and annual meetings. He was always in the thick of the argument, and he argued vigorously and well. He believed strongly in the conclusions he had reached, stated them forthrightly and goodhumoredly, and won most of the battles that he entered. One notable debate that eventually ended in his favor occurred in 1936. It was over the appropriateness of publishing papers on acculturation (cultural change resulting from close contact between peoples) in the *American Anthropologist*. To take another example, it was not easy to launch the program of African studies that Herskovits had envisioned. In time, he overcame the skepticism of a number of faculty members and administrators at Northwestern University who thought his interest in Africa was rather specialized and remote (Prior, 1963).

Among some colleagues at Northwestern and elsewhere, Herskovits had a reputation of being difficult, but others say that as far as they are concerned this reputation was undeserved. Whatever differences of opinion Herskovits had with professional anthropologists, these seem not to have been mentioned to students. Former students assert that Herskovits spoke critically of many of the leading figures in the field in his cultural dynamics and theory courses, but that this was done without personal animus. At the same time, Herskovits' own views were fair game and students were free to attack them. On this point, one anthropologist trained at Northwestern comments: "One of the things we cherished in him was his extraordinary openness to criticism—within the framework of the seminar—of his own approach. His theoretical seminars were very exciting arenas of intellectual give and take."

Herskovits did keep a fairly tight rein on his students, and when some of them became colleagues there was some resentment of his protective hand. He was not, however, a man who held private grudges against those juniors who dared to disagree with him concerning departmental matters or in the intellectual field. One associate recalls receiving a blistering letter attacking a paper he had sent Herskovits from abroad. This colleague—who paid no attention to the criticism, got the paper published, and continued his own work —remarks that "we lived in peace with each other." In dedicating a major scholarly publication to Herskovits, a prominent anthropologist who was a former student and colleague refers to him as "a considerate chairman, helpful colleague, and staunch friend." Another prominent anthropologist, also a former student, wrote in a biographical memoir that "those who had had the privilege of knowing him personally will never forget his warm and vibrant personality." To another colleague, "Mel is a great man, a lovely man, and a man who has left behind him in those who have had intimate association with him a permanent good feeling." Herskovits elicited admiration and loyalty from many who knew him in capacities other than that of professor. For instance, a European scholar regarded him as "a sort of ideal type of non-authoritarian master."

The differences that Herskovits had with a number of prominent anthropologists were characterized in some instances by fireworks in public, but he considered most of these arguments as professional matters. Among these debates were those with Leslie White about cultural evolution, with British anthropologists concerning the functionalist approach in ethnology, with others about the possibilities of applying anthropological knowledge to practical affairs or the desirability of using a neutral term such as nonliterate rather than the term primitive to refer to peoples described in ethnological studies. Some of Herskovits' disagreements with other anthropologists became more personal. Those with George P. Murdock are notable. Their differences had to do with the reorganization of the American Anthropological Association, Murdock's plans for the Human Relations Area Files, Murdock's book on Africa, Herskovits' textbooks (Murdock, 1955, 1302-3), and, quite probably, other matters. The failure of a scholar of Herskovits' eminence ever to be elected president of the American Anthropological Association is attributed by some anthropologists to the positions he took professionally and the manner in which he took them.

According to some who were close to the Herskovitses, Mrs. Herskovits tended to be more concerned about matters affecting Mel's career than he was. She objected to what she thought was injustice to his work, mainly to lack of recognition of his contributions. For example, the Wenner-Gren Foundation Conference, which resulted in a book under Alfred Kroeber's editorship called *Anthropology Today*, did not include a contribution by Herskovits. Those who were familiar with his work shared the indignation of the Herskovitses at that glaring omission. Melville and Frances Herskovits resented anti-Semitism in the United States, and both felt that he was not given his share of recognition in part because of prejudice.

Melville Herskovits was a fascinating and complicated person: brilliant, but at times obdurate; competitive, but extremely generous to friends; confident when he was in full control of a situation, but sometimes insecure when he felt he was not; amiable, witty, and salty, but disdainful of those who did not meet his standards or who disagreed with him on questions about which he felt strongly. In a person of Herskovits' stature, the listing of biographical facts and personality tendencies is overshadowed by his intellectual achieve-

7

ments, his devotion to his field of study, and his integrity. A wide range of interests, great productivity, and humanitarianism, based on the facts of research, marked his work (Merriam, 1964, 83). A colleague asserts that "he knew about all fields of anthropology as none of us who came after him do. He was the last of the all-inclusive anthropologists."

Herskovits is often referred to as a pioneer in the two broad areas in which his later work was centered—Afroamerican Studies and African Studies. The fact is that he was virtually the founder of scientific studies in these fields in the United States. His tireless efforts, his way of conducting research, and the harmonious relationships he established in Africa and the Caribbean were of the greatest importance for the work of later researchers (Hsu and Merriam, 1963, 92; Merriam, 1964, 87). In tracing the link between Africa and the New World, Herskovits dispelled the myth that Afroamericans have no past (Mintz, 1964, 43), and thus vitalized a subject "to which American scholars had been strangely anesthetized and which American Negroes had in the main tended to shun" (Diamond, 1960, 1086).

Herskovits' anthropological interests included music and art, economics, psychology, theoretical formulations, and the application of anthropological knowledge to practical affairs. In all of these areas, as well as in his lifelong devotion to African and Afroamerican studies, he made important contributions. As early as 1936, Herskovits questioned the assumptions that underlie the call for direct applications of anthropological knowledge. He never ceased to believe that "the debt we owe the society that supports us must be made in terms of longtime payments, in our fundamental contributions toward an understanding of the nature and processes of culture, and through this, to the solution of some of our own basic problems" (1936a, 222).

Throughout his career, Herskovits tried to combat the confusions which are rampant in the United States and in the world concerning the biological, social, and cultural aspects of race. Reports on his own research bearing on these matters were supplemented by book reviews, radio addresses, public lectures, and articles in encyclopedias and newspapers. In 1929, 1930, 1932, and 1933 he reviewed the previous year's developments in race relations for the *American Journal of Sociology*. His article on native self-government appeared in 1944 (1944c, 413–24), his "Statement on Africa" was presented at the Hearings before the Committee on Foreign Relations, United States Senate, Eighty-fifth Congress, Second Session, 1958, and he gave similar testimony in 1960. In 1959, he prepared an extensive report, with recommendations on "United States Foreign Policy in Africa," for the Committee on Foreign Relations of the United States Senate.

Field research is the lifeblood of anthropology. Herskovits' field work took Frances and him first to Surinam (Dutch Guiana) in 1928, and at various times from then until 1962 to sub-Saharan Africa, Haiti, Brazil, and Trinidad. Dr. Elsie Clews Parsons, a prominent folklorist, suggested Surinam as a fruitful area for research into Africanisms in the Western Hemisphere, and she provided financial support for the Herskovitses' first field trip. During the first summer in Surinam, they accompanied Dr. Morton C. Kahn of Cornell University Medical College, who had had earlier experience in the colony. An initial grant from Dr. Parsons was the major element in financing the Herskovitses' field trip to Dahomey. Franz Boas sponsored the Surinam project and the research in Dahomey and obtained further financial support for both trips. The results of these studies are to be found in the scores of articles and books published by the Herskovitses over a period of more than thirty years. Throughout Herskovits' career, Frances played the important roles of research associate and colleague. She was the coauthor of a number of articles and of four books: *Rebel Destiny, Suriname Folk-Lore, Trinidad Village,* and *Dahomean Narrative*. Margaret Mead provides an interesting description given to her by Frances Herskovits of the way she and Herskovits wrote *Rebel Destiny*. Each wrote first drafts of half the chapters and then rewrote the other set of chapters. Mead comments: "It was a magnificently written book, and shows no internal signs of such a unique form of authorship." (Personal communication from Margaret Mead, April 12, 1973.) In 1966, she edited a volume of papers by Herskovits titled *The New World Negro: Selected Papers in Afroamerican Studies*.

Herskovits derived his greatest pride and joy from his students. He supported them wholeheartedly, and he lived to see them take their places on the faculties of colleges and universities throughout the world. Their scholarly contributions, especially in the fields of African Studies and Afroamerican Studies, stand as a tribute and as a memorial to his work and his spirit. Among those in this group are William R. Bascom, Joseph H. Greenberg, Alan P. Merriam, Hugh H. Smythe, James W. Fernandez, J. Gus Liebenow, Peter B. Hammond, Robert A. Lystad, Simon Ottenberg, Harold K. Schneider, John C. Messenger, Daniel J. Crowley, Richard A. Waterman, Erika Bourguignon, J. S. Harris, René Ribeiro, James H. Vaughan, Warren L. d'Azevedo, Igor Kopytoff, Philip E. Leis, James B. Christensen, Vernon R. Dorjahn, Robert P. Armstrong, Arthur Tuden, Lowell D. Holmes, David W. Ames, Norman A. Scotch, Alvin W. Wolfe, Phoebe Vestal Miller, John H. Hamer, Joseph G. Moore, Nancy J. Schmidt, Johnnetta B. Cole, and Margaret Katzin. Among those who were not his students but who received special field training from him and were strongly influenced by him were Katherine Dunham, Ralph J. Bunche, and George E. Simpson.

All who knew Mel well spoke of his likeable personal qualities. He was "a rounded personality, full of verve and zest and viewing people with affection and good humor" (Wild, 1963). He was a scientist, but he did not remain aloofly detached from human beings and human affairs. "On the contrary," Prior said, "his warmth, his friendliness, his honesty, and his enthusiasm were great assets to him as a scholar" (1963). Most of the time his energy seemed unlimited, and his ebullience buoyed up the courage of many students and colleagues in their moments of doubt.

Melville J. Herskovits was an illustrious and versatile scholar, an innovator in the field of anthropology, a distinguished and stimulating teacher, a helpful counselor, and a delightful human being. This book is an attempt to present a profile of his scientific work and contributions.

II AFRICA

In 1923, the year in which he was awarded his doctorate, Melville Herskovits published his first article in the *American Anthro-*

pologist on "Some Property Concepts and Marriage Customs of the Vandau." This early interest in Africa stemmed from Professor Franz Boas' "little flurry of inquiry into the Vandau, resulting from a fortuitous acquaintance with an African student at Columbia" (Diamond, 1960, 1086). (Boas published a note in the *Zeitschrift für Ethnologie* in 1921 on "The Concept of Soul Among the Vandau," followed the next year by an article in the same journal on "Das Vervandtschaftssystem der Vandau.")

In his next publication on Africa, Herskovits mapped its culture areas in a preliminary way (1924, 50–64). This attempt grew out of his study of the East African cattle complex and was designed to test on another continent the culture-area concept that Wissler had developed for North American Indian cultures. It was suggested that "by dividing the continent . . . into the nine areas sketched . . . it will be found that the chaos a study of Africa ordinarily presents is greatly reduced" (1924, 63). Revisions of this mapping were made in 1930 and in 1946, and were elaborated upon in 1962 (*Human Factor,* 54–79; see cultural areas map). In its revised form, this cultural map of Africa consisted of nine areas: 1. Khoisan—a. Bushman, b. Hottentot; 2. East African Cattle Area; 3. East Horn; 4. Congo; 5. Guinea Coast; 6. Western Sudan; 7. Eastern Sudan; 8. Desert Area; 9. Egypt. The North African coastal strip was excluded because of its close cultural relationships to Europe, and attention was concentrated on the six culture areas south of the Sahara. Nearly forty years after the first mapping, Herskovits said that the major outlines of these areas "may still be discerned, despite the subsequent impact of Europe" (1962a, 56). The relatively indefinite boundaries of the culture areas do not correspond with those of tribal groups, colonial territories, or the borders of the independent states of the postcolonial period.

Herskovits' doctoral dissertation, "The Cattle Complex in East Africa," was published in four installments in the *American Anthropologist* in 1926. In this study, the available data were reviewed to ascertain the existence of cattle, their place in the life of their owners, the resemblances and differences among the tribes living in the area, as well as those outside its borders where cattle were not found, or where they played different roles in these cultures (1926b, 247 ff.).

As noted earlier, another purpose of the study was to test the applicability of the culture-area concept to a continent other than North America. Special attention was given in the study of the East African cattle area to the importance of cattle in marriage.

Herskovits was one of the first American anthropologists to do field work in Africa. Perhaps one of the reasons that he chose Dahomey, a French-speaking area, was the Herskovitses' facility in French. Frances Herskovits states that Herskovits' field experience in Surinam in 1928 and 1929 "had a profound influence on his think-

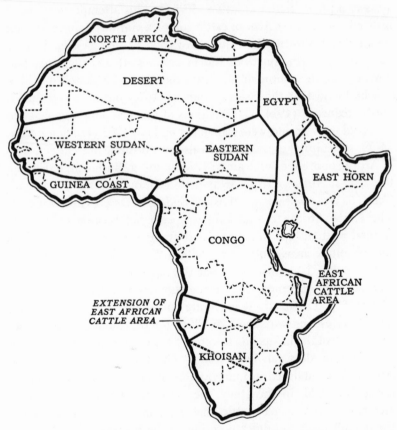

CULTURE AREAS OF AFRICA

Source: M. J. Herskovits, *The Human Factor in Changing Africa*, New York, Alfred A. Knopf, 1962, p. 57.

12

ing. . . . The findings . . . began shaping his concepts on acculturation" (1966, vii). The Dahomean field trip in 1931 seems to have had
an equally strong effect on the direction of Herskovits' career and the
development of Afroamerican studies. Mrs. Herskovits asserts that
the field work in Africa, followed by research in Haiti, "opened up
broader horizons, with new hypotheses to be tested in the laboratory
of Afroamerican cultures" (*ibid.*, viii).

In their field work in Surinam, West Africa, Haiti, Trinidad, and
Brazil, the Herskovitses made extensive use of the participant observer method. In Dahomey, for example, their house in Abomey
was close to the marketplace and permitted easy access to daily
events of interest. Other techniques that they used in field work
included direct observation, talking with a wide range of informants,
the genealogical method, mapping, and the collection of biographical
data. Those who have followed the Herskovitses in the field testify
to the success they had in establishing rapport with members of all
segments of a community. In their division of labor, Frances Herskovits obtained data pertaining to the subculture of the women, as well
as information on some aspects of ritual, art, and other major activities. The Herskovitses' knowledge of French and Portuguese was of
great value in their work in Haiti, Surinam, and Brazil, both with
standard- and nonstandard-language-speaking informants. In Surinam, a phonetic orthography was used in taking down *taki-taki*, or
Negro-English, texts in the city of Paramaribo. In translating these
texts, as well as proverbs in Saramakan, the Negro-Portuguese and
English language of the Bush-Negro, the Herskovitses "retained as
much of the idiom and sentence structure as would not do too much
violence to simple English constructions" (Herskovits and Herskovits,
1936, 117). In the Dahomean study, interpreters were used.

On the basis of field work undertaken in Dahomey in 1931, the
Herskovitses published "An Outline of Dahomean Religious Belief"
as Memoir 41 of the American Anthropological Association in 1933.
This monograph was followed in 1938 by Herskovits' comprehensive
two-volume publication, *Dahomey: An Ancient West African Kingdom.* In addition to analyzing the culture of a part of West Africa,
this publication was intended "to provide materials for those students

13

of New World Negro culture who wish to know more fully the mode of life of the peoples from whom were drawn the ancestors of the Negroes who today inhabit the Americas" (1938b, 1:iii). We refer here to two parts of this seminal work—religion and art.

In the religious life of the Dahomeans, the three major categories of belief pertain to the Great Gods, the ancestors, and personal gods and forces. Of the three groupings of the Great Gods—the public deities—those of the sky pantheon rank first, followed by the Earth pantheon and the Thunder deities. Concerning the gods of the Sky pantheon, Herskovits wrote:

> To the gods of the Sky pantheon, as to all other deities, men and women come to ask for aid in projected undertakings, vowing children to their service if these are successful, while if childless, they come to these gods to ask for offspring, for the Sky gods' role in the lives of their devotees differs neither in kind nor degree from those of the Earth or Thunder. As with all the Great Gods, they are farther removed from the exigencies of daily existence than are such supernatural characters as Legba or Fa [Destiny], or such forces as those which protect by the use of magic, and the essentially ecclesiastical character of Dahomean worship has tended to widen the distance between the gods of all pantheons and the immediate concerns of the individual. Daily communing is most often had with the powers who may be worshipped with a certain degree of spontaneity; and in the worship of the Great Gods spontaneity is the aspect least encouraged. (1938b, 2:128)

In everyday affairs, then, the place of the gods of the Sky pantheon was seen as "neither more nor less important than the place held by any of the Great Gods, whether of Sky, Earth, Sea, or Thunder."

As a group, the Earth deities have two main functions: first, to give to man maize, millet, and other grains of the earth; second, to punish human beings with illnesses, especially with smallpox, when they commit offenses. Like deities of the Sky and Thunder pantheons, these deities grant favors to those who worship them and are in their good graces.

The principal deities of the Thunder pantheon control the various forms of lightning with which they punish. One important Thunder deity has established himself in the sea, and, with his offspring, directs affairs on earth. The overlapping of the functions and the prerogatives, as well as the interrelationships of the gods of the Sky, Earth, and Thunder pantheons, are related by Herskovits (1938b, vol. 2, chapters 26–28).

Considerable detail is presented in *Dahomey* on the organization of worship of the Great Gods (1938b, vol. 2, chapter 29). On the nature of the Dahomean religious experience, Herskovits reported:

> *Skeptics among the Dahomeans themselves state that many of the vodunsi derive nothing deeper from their experience in the cult-house than the enjoyment of freedom from routine and, after emergence, the pleasure of appearing before their acquaintances in the fineries of a cult-member. It is also said that particularly in the case of women is it advantageous to have gone through the initiatory rites of the cult-house, because this gives a woman certain advantages in her relation to the other members of her family, and a certain favorable position with her husband. It is said, further, that some go through the initiatory experience merely to satisfy curiosity. Yet even skeptics admit that there are some who experience the real "mystery" .that is the vodu. Such persons feel an exaltation, a sense of awe and of unity with the god that, though held in check between ceremonies, wells forth at once if the proper songs or drum rhythms are heard. On such occasions, as the vodunsi stand ready to dance, a figure taller than any human stands before them, the left hand outstretched to touch their heads. This is the vodu. And when the hand touches them, they feel a great strength. As they dance, they are no longer themselves, and they remember nothing of what happened when the vodu finally leaves them. But when they regain consciousness of the world outside, and are themselves once more, they feel as though something heavy had left them. (1938b, 2:199–200)*

In traditional Dahomean culture, the ancestral cult was the "focal point" of social organization (1938b, 1:194). For a sib and its subdivisions to continue to exist and to prosper, the worship of its ancestors had to be faithfully observed. Important aspects of the cult of the dead included the conclusion of funeral ceremonies for all dead adults within three years after their death to prevent the loss of souls to the sib, and the deification of the ancestors at intervals of one or more decades. All Dahomeans believed their ancestors stood between them and the gods that personified the forces of the universe that threatened periodically to destroy them.

In one sense, the third division of Dahomean religious beliefs—the personal gods and forces—provided a link between the beliefs concerning the ancestral cult and those concerning the great "public" deities (1938b, 2:201). The principal personal forces and gods were Fa, or Destiny as willed by the gods; Legba, the official linguist or messenger who transmitted to the various deities the orders given by Fate; Da, a vodu that "incarnates the quality of dynamics in life . . . movement, flexibility, sinuousness, fortune" and that manifests itself "as a serpent, as rainbow, as umbilicus, as plant roots, as the nerves of animal forms, as the gaseous emanations that issue from mountains" (*ibid.*, 255). Others of the principal spiritual forces were the three souls of man, a man's shadow, and the ancestral guardian soul which is transmitted to a man's descendants. All aspects of a system of divination that enables the diviner to ascertain the will of destiny are subsumed under the term Fa, a system derived from Ifa divination of the Yoruba in Ife, Nigeria. (Other types of divination exist alongside Fa.) In the Fa system, the diviner foretells the future by using appropriate myths to interpret the combinations obtained by throwing sixteen palm nuts. Fa must be worshipped by all men, each of whom must obtain his own Destiny. Although a man's fate is foreordained by Fa, the power that may permit him to escape his destiny is Legba, the divine trickster whose intrigues are carried on even against the most powerful gods.

Herskovits pointed out incisively the close relationships between religion and art in Dahomey, emphasizing especially the embellishment of cult objects, the decoration of the persons and clothing of those who dance for the gods, and the development of song and dance in the rites performed for the deities. He did not neglect, however, the nonreligious elements of Dahomean art as found in economic, social, and political life. Also, the useful arts were distinguished from the nonuseful, the latter applying particularly to the graphic and plastic arts. In making this distinction, Herskovits differed from some scholars in the fields of art and of anthropology who had held that nonliterate peoples create only art that is intended for definite ends. Some Dahomean art was produced for those who could afford objects of beauty for pleasure—wall hangings to adorn the walls of the homes of chiefs, some wood carvings, and some brass figures (1938b, 2:313–14). Herskovits found that specific criteria of good and bad art existed in Dahomey, especially in connection with brass pieces and appliqué cloths, but that "these criteria are set up and maintained by persons of artistic sophistication, by individuals whose tastes have been trained to recognize and appreciate artistic excellence, rather than by the populace . . ." (*ibid.,* 316). Of exceptional interest is the following succinct, insightful observation on wood carving:

> The most democratic of the graphic and plastic arts is wood-carving, for any man may be a wood-carver. This does not imply that there are no carvers who make it their special calling. In at least one compound in Abomey a number of the inhabitants are wood-carvers by hereditary right. Many men prefer to make their own carvings, however, even though the product may be aesthetically deficient. For wood-carving, more than any of the other arts, is associated with religion, and the essence of a gbo is that its power not be dissipated by something placed in it designedly or unwittingly by its maker. This is the reason why there is so much greater variation both in style and in degree of excellence in wood-carving than in any of the other arts. (1938b, 2:316)

According to Herskovits, the two most significant forms of Dahomean plastic art are the work in brass and wood, but iron objects and bas-reliefs in clay are also found (1938b, 2:354; and see selections 1 and 2 in this volume). The process used in brass working is the lost-wax method of direct casting. The figures made by the brass workers for Dahomeans, particularly those acquired by the chiefs, were of the finest quality, while those made for export showed a certain amount of degeneration. In style, the brass castings represented a combination of realism and conventionalization (*ibid.*, 359–61).

In Dahomey, the two principal types of graphic art were the appliqué cloths and the incised calabashes (see selection 1 in this volume). The symbolism of the calabash carvings was employed mainly to convey love messages from men to women and their use was restricted to the members of the leisure class. Appliqué work had much wider uses; some examples were the state umbrellas covered with designs, the caps of chiefs, the banners of nonrelationship groupings such as secret societies and mutual aid associations, and decorated cloths used in the worship of the gods (1938b, 2:328). Herskovits took exception to the position of some students that nonliterate art is less subject to change than the arts of literate peoples. Citing evidence of changes in composition of Dahomean appliqué designs, he demonstrated that following the prevalent patterns of a given art in a particular culture does not prevent the artist from making changes based on his own perceptions (*ibid.*, 337–40). A lesser form of Dahomean art comprised mural painting, usually employed to decorate the walls of religious temples. These were "crude in design and execution" and were found in the temples devoted to children born with anomalous physical characteristics—six-fingered children, four-fingered children, stillborn and aborted children, hermaphroditic types, malformed children, and misshapen births (*ibid.*, 343–44).

In a 1955 article, "Peoples and Cultures of Sub-Saharan Africa," Herskovits reviewed the basic cultural orientations of African peoples, but drew a contrast between the pastoral societies of the East African Cattle Area, the Eastern Sudan, and those southern and western portions of the East Horn that are not dominated culturally by the literate Amharic groups, and the agricultural societies of the Congo, Guinea Coast, and Western Sudan areas. In explaining these differences, the ecological factor was emphasized—the high, dry plains on the one hand and the lower-lying forested area on the other (1955b, 15–18). In the agricultural societies, specialization of labor encouraged trade, markets, and the development of pecuniary units of value. Likewise, these developments facilitated commercial and cultural contacts. Specialization also occasioned stratification and a social class structure. In short, the agricultural region was seen as one "of stable kingdoms, of established priesthoods and explicit theological systems maintained by those specialists in government and in the manipulation of the supernatural that only economies capable of producing substantial surpluses over subsistance needs can carry in the highly developed forms found in this region" (*ibid.*, 18–19). The differences between these two major cultural provinces were said to have been significant in the adjustments of their peoples to European contact. The relative ease of West Africans and the peoples of the Congo in taking over the growing of cash crops was contrasted with the difficulty the eastern pastoral peoples had in utilizing their herds commercially and in adopting methods of raising the quality of their domesticated animals. Also, the agriculturalists had less difficulty adjusting to the pecuniary system of the world economic order than did the pastoralists. Despite the differences between culture areas and principal geographical regions, this article points out the underlying unities of sub-Saharan Africa, including unilateral descent systems, the religious importance of the ancestors and the respect for the senior members of any grouping, the traditions of the age-grades and the puberty school which have predisposed Africans to formal training in literacy, the concept of land tenure that vests ownership of land in the community and gives the individual control over it only during its occupancy and use, the pluralistic world view that has contributed to the receptivity to Christianity and Islam, the techniques of social control through satire, and the role of magic.

In 1959, Bascom and Herskovits edited a series of studies by anthropologists trained at Northwestern University. This book was a good example of Herskovits' devotion to his students and his interest in furthering their work. In the Introduction, the editors comment on cultural continuity and change in Africa (Bascom and Herskovits, 1959, 2–6). It is noted that there are strong contrasts among African cultures in the extent to which Euroamerican innovations have been accepted or rejected. Religion is a case in point. Although Moslem proselytizing has gone on for thousands of years and Christian missionaries have carried on extensive programs, African religious beliefs and practices have not disappeared. In the post-World War II period, many Africans continued to worship African deities, and homage to the ancestors, as well as recourse to divination, magic, and other rituals, was very much in evidence. The fact that many Africans have accepted new religious beliefs did not mean that African religious traditions were about to vanish. In the contemporary African scene, Bascom and Herskovits said that selection is often additive rather than substitutive. Among the examples cited in support of this point are (1) the severe competition of European machine-made gods has not eliminated African weavers, smiths, and potters; (2) the desire for literacy can be satisfied without inducing cultural conflict; (3) the acceptance of the deity of another people may mean that the new deity is added to the supernatural resources available for assistance.

Herskovits' last book, *The Human Factor in Changing Africa*, illustrates his interest in the application of anthropological theory to the understanding of contemporary problems of culture change in Africa. In some degree, this interest grew out of the association of a number of African political leaders with the Program of African Studies at Northwestern University, together with the many friendships with Africans that the Herskovitses formed in the United States and in Africa. Among these leaders were Leopold Sédar Senghor of Senegal, William V. S. Tubman of Liberia, Kwame Nkrumah of Ghana, Nnamdi Azikiwe of Nigeria, Sékou Touré of Guinea, Eduardo Mondlane of Mozambique, Tom Mboya of Kenya, and K. A. Busia of Ghana. Herskovits also had a wide acquaintance with English and French colonial officials, and with European and African scholars. Many of these persons came to Northwestern University to lead seminar discussions and to confer with him.

Especially noteworthy in *The Human Factor* are the discussions of the city, the school, and the search for values. The cities of eastern and southern Africa—more European in their planning, appearance, and organization, and requiring a greater degree of adjustment on the part of their residents—are contrasted with the pattern of urbanization, based on indigenous urban settlements, found in West Africa (1962a, 262). Despite these differences, the city in every part of the continent became a major aspect of African cultures. New administrative and trading centers arose, as did towns based on coal, iron, and copper mining. In some cases, hamlets of a few dozen or a few hundred people grew within twenty or thirty years to places of 15,000 or 20,000.

Studies of migratory movements were used to show the problems of adjustment to life in the city and the repercussions of these movements in the rural areas from which the migrants came. A migrant who came to work in the mines in South Africa was discouraged from bringing his family with him. In West Africa, the migrant was a free agent, able to come and go as he pleased and to move from one kind of work to another. In some parts of Africa, pass systems controlled movements from one section of a country to another and in South Africa, regulations restricted the type of work an African might obtain in the city (1962a, 276).

The usual problems of urbanization were found in Africa, but these problems took on a special character:

> Here city dwellers not only had to solve the usual problems of urban life everywhere—questions of housing, of health and hygiene, of recreation, of juvenile delinquency—but the complexity of these problems was compounded by other factors. In the areas of permanent non-African settlement, city life sharpened a sense of differentials based on race, on standards of living, on education, on economic opportunity and the like, since in the city these were experienced at close range, and thereby served to multiply the frictions arising out of continuous propinquity. Even where multiracial tensions were minimal, the rapidity with which those who migrated to the towns had to adapt themselves to life in the new setting introduced special problems into what is at best a difficult enough process, even in those parts of the world where the city in its later forms had long been known. (1962a, 286)

Herskovits distinguished clearly between change and demoralization in the study of urbanization in Africa. In addition, he stressed the importance of recognizing that some aspects of culture, particularly values such as music or language and those elements which exist beneath the level of consciousness, are less susceptible to change than material culture and technology (1962a, 294).

Another aspect of urbanization dealt with incisively by Herskovits is the widespread retention of belief in magic, in the efficacy of aboriginal medicine, and in divination (1962a, 295–96). Even in industrialized districts, psychological insecurity has strengthened these beliefs. Of especial interest is the reinterpretation of indigenous belief, the result of which is that many Africans seek the services of both European physicians and local doctors and diviners.

For centuries, Africans had trained their children in ways of getting a living, in morals, in religious rituals, and in creative expression—graphic and plastic arts, the dance, and oral narrative. Much of this training was given informally, but indigenous instruction also included the apprenticeship system and initiation rites.

Although educational policies differed from country to country during the colonial period, the desire for schooling grew steadily. Since formal teaching was concerned with matters outside the indigenous cultures, the African child had to make many adjustments in school and in later life. Questions arose concerning whether an African or a European language should be used in instruction, but of even greater importance was the tendency "to write off aboriginal beliefs, moral codes and other regulatory social devices, along with material culture and native technology, as being of a quality that deserved little or no attention in planning curricula or classroom procedures for African schools" (1962a, 221). Until the middle 1950s, little attention was paid to the practice of ignoring African culture in the schools. Nevertheless, schooling provided Africans with resources for meeting the changing world: a language which enabled them to move into the European academic system, and a procedure for evaluating the elements in the two worlds to which they had been exposed.

Although school programs were consonant with colonial policy throughout sub-Saharan Africa, political controls outside the Portuguese territories and South Africa were relatively light. In the latter areas government control of teaching and of extracurricular activities was explicit, and Africans had no voice in the administration of educational policy (1962a, 230–32). The Portuguese and the South Africans differed in the ends they sought through education for Africans. The former said their policy was one of the eventual absorption of the African into the Portuguese way of life; the latter aimed at forcing Africans to return to aboriginal ways and then embarking on a path of separate development under European control. Both aims were unrealistic.

Herskovits pointed out the importance of the role played by Christian missions in introducing formal education, adding that many Africans came to prefer secular schooling. In part, this preference was based on missionary disapproval in the classroom of many aspects of African life that continued to be highly esteemed. Under special circumstances, Africans preferred mission schools. One example was the taking over of such schools in South Africa to further the policy of apartheid (1962a, 247–48).

To round out his account of formal education in sub-Saharan Africa, Herskovits summarized the establishment of university colleges, institutes of technology, and independent universities during the first fifteen years of the post-World War II period. Among the problems at that time of making higher education available to Africans were the Africanization of staff, the maintenance of objective standards of scholarship during a period of developing nationalisms, and adapting curricula to African requirements (1962a, 252–56).

One of the most original sections of *The Human Factor in Changing Africa* deals with "the search for values." Herskovits' insight is at its best in passages like the following:

> *Values in aboriginal African society must be inferred from African behavior, African social institutions, African beliefs. These values are never systematically formulated. They are most explicit in the proverbs and moralizing tales, which reveal a system of ethical principles, once the hidden meaning of all aphorisms, and the patterns of their use, are analyzed in cultural context. In some societies the values found in these forms have a high degree of complexity, and cover approved behavior in many different kinds of situations. . . . (1962a, 465–66)*

23

Three values stood out in the discussions of Africans concerning new African ideologies: (1) the traditional rights and obligations of members of kinship groups, (2) respect for one's elders, (3) the value of cooperative effort. Another aspect of African behavior, "implicit in traditional narrative and reinforced by the experience of conquest, colonial or indigenous," that was not lost sight of was the principle of circumspection in dealing with strangers and superiors (1962a, 466). Also, values associated with traditional graphic and plastic arts gained the esteem of educated Africans. These values, taken together, affirmed the fundamental principle of "the continuity of experience, under which the past, the present and the future are conceived to be a unified whole" (*ibid.*).

Among the values derived from contact which were widely accepted were the greater emphasis on a pecuniary economy, on nearly all aspects of technological change, and on many types of non-African material goods—"roads, bridges, motor cars, multistoried buildings, power dams. . . ." In addition, the values placed upon literacy and the recognition of political independence in international affairs were generally accepted. On the other hand, some of the new values, especially several in the area of internal political organization, were in conflict with old values. Values based on age and hereditary status clashed with systems of political democracy as well as with the idea of strict one-party control. African leaders, both where patterns of individual effort had become established and where "African socialism" was being advocated, reexamined traditional communal patterns as they sought to promote economic growth and higher living standards (1962a, 467).

Two value-laden concepts were used in the 1950s and early 1960s to reestablish the authenticity of African cultures and to emphasize the validity of the African position internationally. These "myths" were those of "negritude" and the "African personality." The former concept was employed mainly in the French-speaking nations, the latter was more popular in the English-speaking countries, especially in Ghana (1962a, 468–70).

In his final publication on Africa, Herskovits emphasized the theme of continuity and change in African customs.

Life and Work

Because my scientific orientation, without neglecting the institutions that provide the structural framework of social life, is directed toward people, this book stresses the human factor in assessing the developments that have marked Africa. In treating of these developments, my primary emphasis is on the reactions of the peoples of Africa to the situations which they have had to meet. . . . Critical here is the study of the way in which conservatism, the retention of established custom, and change, the acceptance of innovation, have interacted. (1962a, vii–ix)

Assessments of Herskovits' African studies have stressed the realistic picture he presented of Dahomean culture (Wieschhoff, 1939, 623), the way he combined a scientific with a humanistic approach (Schneider, 1963, 27), and his thorough and ramifying concern with Africa (Diamond, 1960, 1086). Until the end of his life, he was, indeed, the dean of African studies in the United States.

III   THE NEW WORLD NEGRO

Introduction. With the end of the slave trade and slavery itself, a gap appeared in the literature concerning the Negro peoples of the Western hemisphere (Mintz, 1964, 43). "Only with the publication of Herskovits' *The Myth of the Negro Past* (1941a)," Mintz says, "did the place of New World Negro peoples become once more a central issue for scholars." In developing his thesis concerning the relationships between African and Afroamerican cultures, Herskovits gave attention to a number of intermediate steps. He cited evidence showing that the greater proportion of the slaves derived from a relatively restricted area, the coastal area of West Africa (1941a, ch. 2). Another point of importance considered in his work was the order of arrival of different tribal groups. Those who came late to the New World had to adjust to the patterns of behavior established by earlier arrivals (1941a, 52).[1] He outlined the cultural

[1] Curtin points out that the Whites were not anxious to force Europeanization any further than was necessary for plantation work. Left to educate their own children, the slaves developed a new culture consisting of the varied elements of the African heritage and some European elements (Curtin, 1955, 25; and see Mintz, 1966a, 922).

25

characteristics of the West African–Congo area: agriculture as the mainstay of the productive economy, with the addition of herding in the northern savanna country; hoe-culture; cooperative labor to break the soil; ownership of land by larger relationship groups; division of labor by crafts and the presence of family guilds; unilineal and patrilocal social organization; polygyny; power of the elders based on closeness of their relationship to the ancestors; secret societies at both ends of the area; variation in political organization from large kingdoms to small autonomous units; universality of the institution of courts; conception of the universe as ruled by Great Gods; divination; sacredness of ancestors; magic; role of song and dance in daily life; importance of percussion units; complex rhythm; leader-chorus singing; importance of graphic and plastic arts; and the prevalence of tales, proverbs, and riddles (*ibid.*, 81–85). To those who asked how the Africans, coming from different tribes and speaking different languages, could communicate with one another, Herskovits pointed out the common structural base of the West African Sudanese tongues. Dialects were mutually unintelligible because of differences in vocabulary rather than in construction, and mutual understanding became possible after a relatively short period of contact (*ibid.*, 80–81).

Early in his study of New World Negro populations, Herskovits drew distinctions among aspects of African culture which had been retained almost unchanged, those which had been reinterpreted in new settings, and those which had been synthetized in complex ways with non-African beliefs and customs. Where outer form could not be retained, he maintained that it was disregarded while inner values were retained through the processes of reinterpretation or syncretism (1941a, 297–98). Thus the outer forms of Protestantism, which characterize the "shouting" churches of lower-class Negroes in the United States and in the Caribbean, were seen as an overlay on a world view that includes many elements of non-European ritual and theology. One instance of this type of religious adaptation is a belief system in which "the European emphasis on guilt and punishment for guilt have been rejected in favor of African religious affirmations" (1951a, 146). Likewise, in the realm of the family, new outer forms have been accepted but reinterpreted in terms of the patterns of older traditions.

26

To assist in classifying the materials of New World Negro cultures, Herskovits drew up a scale of intensity of Africanisms which ranged the aspects of culture, by country, from the most African to the most European. The greatest degree of retention is seen in music, folklore, religion, and magic, the least in technology and economic life, with language, social organization, and art in intermediate positions. By subareas within countries, the general trend from high to low retention is from the interior of Surinam through Haiti, Brazil (Bahia, Porto Alegre, the urban north, the rural north), Jamaica, Trinidad, Cuba, Honduras (Black Caribs), Virgin Islands, Gulla Islands, to the United States (rural South, North) (1955a, 525–28).

Differences in the degree of retention of African custom in different parts of the New World were hypothesized to be due to climate and topography, the organization and operation of the plantations, the numerical ratios of Negroes to Whites, and whether Negro-white contacts occurred in rural or urban settings (1941a, 111). Herskovits pointed out, for example, that Negroes lived in constant association with Whites in the southern part of the United States to a degree not found elsewhere in the New World. In the plantation areas of the Caribbean and in South America, the "poor white" and the white man with but a few slaves was relatively rare (*ibid.*, 121). As a result of contacts on the plantations between newly arrived Africans and house servants, the latter were exposed to forces that encouraged the retention of African custom (*ibid.*, 133). Urban life did not necessarily mean that the Negroes took over European ways more readily; it might mean that either the retention of Africanisms in modified form or the adoption of European customs would be accelerated (*ibid.*, 121–25). With the passage of time, the degree of reinterpretation varied above all with socioeconomic status. On this point Herskovits was quite explicit: "In those strata of society where there has been full access to the cultural resources of the dominant group, even reinterpreted elements would be idiosyncratic, rarely patterned" (1951a, 145).

From time to time since the publication of *The Myth of the Negro Past*, alternative approaches to the New World Negro concept have been proposed. These rubrics have included Plantation America, race relations, the plural society, and the family and household

27

composition of migratory wage laborers in relation to the larger society (Whitten and Szwed, 1970, 30). Reactions to these alternatives have varied greatly. For example, Mintz says that "the plural society concept, as applied to the Caribbean, has not caught hold widely. . . . Most Caribbeanists have either rejected the term, ignored it, or used it casually" (Mintz, 1966b, 1047). Frazier (1957, v) and Herskovits (1960, 562) criticized the use of the term Plantation-America. Discussions of family, household, matrifocality, and ego-centered kinship networks among Afroamericans, migratory and nonmigratory, abound. In the contemporary world, preoccupation with race relations is widespread, especially in matters of education, politics, jobs, housing, and welfare. Particularly in the United States it is almost impossible for social scientists to think about Blacks [2] without, at the same time, thinking about Whites, and vice versa. In many ways, these controversies have been useful. The question is which conceptualizations are most adequate for a given task.

Herskovits was interested in the cultural totality wherever Afroamericans live, and not simply in "the segments of African forms of behavior and of African institutions that have been retained in the course of the New World experience of the Negro (1952c, 59)." In his view, ". . . what has been taken over from non-African cultures is . . . just as important as what of Africa has been retained . . ." (*ibid.*). His explanation of the behavior and customs of New World Negroes was not based only on the cultural heritage, but included the effects of slavery, and the socioeconomic experiences of Afroamericans since emancipation (1941a, 8, 136).[3]

---

[2] Since the middle 1960s, a sharp controversy has raged over the appropriate term for persons in the New World of African or part-African descent. In the United States, the term "Blacks," formerly one of the least favored names among individuals of African descent, is now one of the most popular. In this book, Black, Negro, and Afroamerican are used interchangeably (when used as nouns, Black and White are capitalized; when used as adjectives they are not). The terms that Herskovits used most frequently were New World Negro and Afroamerican. See Lerone Bennett, Jr. (1970, 379), and Simpson and Yinger (1972, ch. 1).

[3] Mintz distinguishes between a "societal" and a "cultural" approach to the study of Caribbean populations, saying that Pan-Caribbean uniformities "consist largely of parallels of economic and social structure and organization, the

Technology, Economic Life, and Political Organization. African traditions had the least chance to survive in these aspects of culture.

> African draped clothes were replaced by tailored clothing, . . . the short-handled, broad-bladed hoe gave way to the longer-handled, slimmer-bladed implement of Europe; and such techniques as weaving and ironworking and wood carving were almost entirely lost. Except for such poor barter as the slaves could contrive among themselves, or in so far as they were permitted to sell in the markets, no remnant of the economic complexities of Africa remained on the plantation. Such a widespread institution as pawning had no opportunity to function in the New World, nor could more than a few of the most rudimentary devices be carried on outside the all-encompassing dictates of the master. (1941a, 136–37)

The study of the retention of Africanisms in motor habits remains largely undeveloped. Herskovits advocated research in this field through the analysis of motion pictures of such activities as walking, speaking, laughing, sitting postures, burden carrying, hoeing, certain industrial habits, dancing, and singing. In Haiti and in other parts of the New World, Herskovits observed that the tradition of intricate hair-braiding, particularly in the case of small girls, had continued undiminished (1937b, 253). He called attention to a perfect example of the Charleston in a film of ancestral rites in the Ashanti village of Asokore, and to the resemblance to other styles of Negro dancing in the United States included in films made in Dahomey and in southwestern Nigeria. Also, the exact method of planting photographed in Dahomey and in Haiti was seen by Bascom in the Gulla Islands in 1939 (1941a, 145–46; 1937b, 254). Among the industrial techniques that Herskovits reported as African reten-

---

consequence of lengthy and rather rigid colonial rule" (Mintz, 1966a, 914–15). He treats as secondary the fact that many of the component societies of the Caribbean share similar or historically related cultures. Among other scholars who have emphasized the structural approach in Afroamerican studies are E. F. Frazier (1943; 1949, ch. 1), and R. T. Smith (1956, ch. 9). (See "The Family and Domestic Institutions," below.)

tions is the use of the mortar and pestle, together with woven trays used in winnowing rice. The sewing technique called coiling used in making these woven trays on the Sea Islands of Georgia is common in West Africa (1941a, 147).

In Haiti, the type of house found in the countryside is derived from West Africa and from Europe. The African side is seen in the kind of thatching and in the walls of woven withes daubed with mud. The gabled roof and the rectangular floor plan are common to West Africa and to Europe (1937b, 251).

In rural Haiti, African ways of preparing food have been retained with little change. Food is cooked either on a raised mud platform in the cooking shelter or on three stones; both of these methods are used in Africa. At least one dish, *acansan* (cooked balls of cornmeal), has a Nigerian-Dahomean name. White bread has been adopted from European sources, while cassava cakes stem from the aboriginal Indian diet (1937b, 254–55). In Toco, a small village in northern Trinidad, the Herskovitses found a number of dishes that are directly traceable to Africa: sweet and salt *pemi* (boiled cornmeal), *sansam* (parched corn, mixed with salt or sugar), *cachop* (baked cornmeal), *calalu* (a crab and okra stew, with pork fat and grated coconut), and *acra* (boiled salt fish dipped in flour, with hot peppers added, and fried in deep fat using coconut oil). In addition, eating habits are African, with "breakfast" coming in the middle of the morning and the second main meal in the late afternoon. As in Africa, the mother and children do not ordinarily eat with the man of the family (Herskovits and Herskovits, 1947b, 289).

Herskovits argued that the tradition of cooperation, an important part of West African agriculture, has been continued in parts of the New World. Cooperative work groups were cited as "an example of the retention of a custom which was immediately applicable to the requirements of the slave system, where gang labor was the fundamental technique employed in working the estates. Under freedom the older custom merely reasserted itself, to obtain results that were beyond individual effort" (Herskovits and Herskovits, 1947b, 290–91). He saw the *combite* in Haiti as the equivalent of the *dokpwe* in Dahomey. (See selection 3 in this volume.) The carry-overs included the practice of giving a substantial meal at the end of the day instead of pay for the work done, the attitudes of pleasure associated with group work, and the role of singing in setting a rhythm for the work and in exercising social control over the participants (1937b, 257). Other examples of the persistence of the tradition of cooperative work are seen in the tree-felling parties of the Surinam Bush Negroes, the *gayap* in Trinidad, the *troca dia* ("exchange of day's work," similar to a nonrelationship, mutual-aid grouping called *so* in Dahomey) in northern Brazil, and the various forms of group labor in agriculture, fishing, house-raising, and other enterprises in Jamaica and the French West Indies (1941a, 161; Herskovits and Herskovits, 1947b, 290–91).[4]

In Trinidad, as among the Yoruba, a savings device (*esusu* in Nigeria, *susu* in Toco) exists to enable persons to save systematically and the *gbe* and the *so* groupings in Dahomey have similar features. Members deposit a certain sum each week with a functionary who turns over the entire weekly collection to a different participant in the group until all have received their "hands." In Barbados and Guyana this type of association is known respectively as "a meeting" and "boxi money" (1941a, 165; Herskovits and Herskovits, 1947b, 292).

During slavery African political interests and talents were virtually extinguished. During the earlier periods of slavery African traditions of organization were evident in large-scale Negro revolts, but these were exceptional cases (1941a, 137).

The Family and Domestic Institutions. One of the most frequently questioned of Herskovits' conclusions concerning New World Negroes is the relationship he saw between African polygyny and

[4] M. G. Smith has contended that the cooperative factor in Caribbean agricultural pursuits cannot be related to African cultures because the work groups are not parallel in all respects to the African model of the *dokpwe* (M. G. Smith, 1957, 44). Here again is seen the disagreement between those who regard reinterpretation of African traditions as an important part of the acculturative process and those who demand the revelation of African cultural traits in pure form as evidence of African influence on New World Negroes (Simpson and Hammond, 1957, 46–53).

Melville J. Herskovits

Caribbean plural marriage. In West Africa, Herskovits contrasted the relationship between father and children against mother and children.

> Where a man has plural wives, the offspring of any one woman must share their father with those of other women, while they share their mother with none but other children by her. This psychological fact is reinforced by the physical setting of family life in this area, as well as by the principles of inheritance of wealth, which obtain at least among the Yoruba and in Dahomey. The family is typically housed in a compound, which is a group of structures surrounded by a wall or a hedge, to give the total complex a physical unity. The head of the household, the eldest male, and all other adult males, married or unmarried (for in some parts of the area young married sons or younger married brothers and their children may live in a father's or elder brother's compound), have individual huts of their own, to which their wives come in turn to live with them and, for a stated period, to care for their needs. Each wife has her own dwelling, however, where she lives with her children. (Herskovits, 1941a, 64-65)

In Haiti, plaçage, a type of mating which does not have Church approval, and in the English-speaking West Indies "keeping" were considered by Herskovits to reflect the African polygynous marriage pattern (1941a, 168).

In the main, Herskovits found that attachments are closer between a mother and her child than those between a father and his children in the Negro family in the United States, the West Indies, and South America, and he argued that the "matriarchal" family type showed the influence of African polygynous tradition (1941a, 169–70). He did not claim that the status of the Negro family was due solely to the continuation of African traditions. Instead, he wrote about "the play of various forces in the New World experience of the Negro, projected against a background of aboriginal tradition" (1941a, 181). His explanation of the "maternal" family found extensively among New World Negroes comprises the African tradition of polygyny and the tradition of a sentimental attachment to

32

the mother; the experiences of persons of African descent during slavery, including the selling of the father away from the rest of the family, and a lack of differentiation between the sexes in exploiting slave labor; the economic independence of women and the necessity of calling on all the labor resources in their families in the period since freedom (1941a, 180–81).

Another domestic institution in the African tradition cited by Herskovits is the "caretaker" arrangement whereby a child is entrusted for rearing, in return for its services, to a family that can provide greater advantages than its own home. Examples of this tradition are seen in the *kweki* practice of Surinam and the *'ti moune* custom of Haiti (Herskovits and Herskovits, 1947b, 290).

In discussing the New World Negro family, Frazier, Raymond Smith, and Michael Smith rely on some type of structural or sociological approach and, in varying degrees, on historical data related to slavery and the postslavery periods (Herskovits, 1960, 565–66).[5] According to Herskovits, earlier, pre-American patterns were reinterpreted by Africans in the process of adapting to conditions in the New World. He argued that even where overt forms of African behavior and customs disappeared, sanctions underlying generalized aspects of West African culture could be discovered. He pointed out the error in assuming that no impulses from Africa have been received in the New World for centuries, as well as the importance of the accommodations that slaves who came late to the New World had to make to patterns of behavior established earlier on the basis

---

[5] According to Herskovits, Frazier's conclusion that the African influence in the Bahian family had disappeared was based only on overt forms and ignored underlying sanctions (Frazier, 1943, 404; Herskovits, 1943b, 395–99). R. T. Smith argues that the Negro matrifocal family in Guyana is "the obverse of the marginal nature of the husband-father role" (R. T. Smith, 1956, 221), but Kreiselman maintains that matrifocality cannot be explained by social and occupational marginality because they are a single unit (Kreiselman, 1957, 913). Another structural analysis of matrifocality attributes the consanguineal household in *neoteric* or "newly created" societies to the financial and psychological security it provides to both the female and the male (González, 1970, 244). M. G. Smith explains the variations in Caribbean mating systems by historical conditions (M. G. Smith, 1962), an explanation that is questioned by Otterbein (1964, 74–76).

33

of the customs of the tribes represented during the middle period of slaving (1941a, 226 and 52).

In short, while Herskovits' strongest interest was in the cultural component, he stressed the point that the behavior and customs of New World Negroes could be understood only in terms of three variables: the background of West African traditions, the conditions of life during slavery, and the socioeconomic status of Afro-Americans since freedom (1941a, 8, 136, 180–81). In their explanations, most of his critics rely on one or both of the latter two variables.

Religion and Related Aspects of Culture. In religion, and in some more or less closely associated activities, the situation during slavery furthered African retentions and reinterpretations. Herskovits quotes with approval Puckett's comment that "the white master was careful to see that American farming practice was followed by the slaves. He cared less about the amusements and religion of the Negro so long as they did not affect his working ability" (Puckett, 1926, 10; quoted in Herskovits, 1941a, 137). Similar attitudes prevailed in other parts of the New World where the system of slavery existed.

In the Caribbean and in those parts of South America where the ratio of persons of African descent in the total population was highest, and where these persons were most severely isolated from those of European descent, the likelihood that African religious traditions would persist in easily recognized form was greatest. Beginning with their field work in Surinam in 1928 and 1929, the Herskovitses reported on many of these retentions (Herskovits and Herskovits, 1936, 44–70). Among the Surinam town Negroes, the six principal groups of *winti* (gods) are of African origin. There were Kromanti (Gold Coast) Thunder gods; Earth gods from the Gold Coast; sacred snakes (derived from Fon and Ashanti [Gold Coast] beliefs); river gods, some of whom entered into the group of snake deities; Kromanti gods, including the vulture, a messenger who took sacrifices to the gods; and the gods of the bush, including the little people of the forest (1941a, 255–58; Herskovits and Herskovits, 1936, 66–67; 1947b, 291–92); and the silk-cotton tree. The latter tree is sacred in West Africa; in Dahomey the souls of ancestors are believed to have

34

resided in them. The little people have their counterparts in Dahomey, among the Yoruba of Nigeria and Dahomey, among the Ashanti, and in Trinidad and Brazil. In addition to these groups, the Herskovitses mention individual gods in Surinam under the heading of "African spirits." Among these is *Leba*, the guardian of the crossroads of West Africa (1941a, 219).[6]

Herskovits' field work in Haiti in 1934 added to materials presented earlier in works by such Haitian writers as Price-Mars (1928) and Dorsainvil (1931) concerning the African aspects of *vodun*. The *vodun* cult in Mirebalais includes such Dahomean deities as Damballa and Legba, and in some instances the word *Dahomey* is a part of a god's name. Many *vodun* gods have Yoruba names, including 'Batala, Ogun, and Shango. Several Congo gods are represented in the cult, as well as deities from Angola and from the Ibo region of Nigeria. The word *vodun* itself is the general term for deity in Dahomey. The root *hun-* in such words as *hungan* (*vodun* priest) and *hunsi* (a cult initiate) is Dahomean, where it is synonymous with *vodun*. *Gan* is the Dahomean word for chief, and *si* means wife (1937b, 267–68). Herskovits saw the use of the *images* (portraits of the saints) as "the outward symbol of the psychological reconciliation that has been effected between the saints of the Church and the African deities" (*ibid.*, 278–79). The disparities between the equating of Catholic saints and African gods among Negroes in different countries in the New World indicated, he thought, that these syncretizations had developed independently in each region where they occurred (1937a, 643).

The African tradition of sacrifice plays a prominent part in *vodun* (1937b, 269) and in other New World Negro cults. As in West Africa, "feeding" the gods is one means of trying to insure that a deity, who is capable of doing both good and evil to its followers, will provide protection and favors.

Herskovits concluded that the death rites in Haiti included African elements (1937b, 259–60). Acknowledging that the outer forms of the ancestral cult in West Africa had disappeared, he argued that the meticulous manner of performing the rituals for the dead, and

[6] For a recent report on the Winti in Surinam, see Wooding (1972, 51–78).

Melville J. Herskovits

particularly the institution of *mangé morts*, indicated that the spirit of African customs had survived. After mass at the Catholic Church and a reception at the home of a relative in town, members of the family and friends returned to the habitation in the country for a *mangé* (feast) and dances (European and *vodun*).

The important role played by the spirits of the dead in a number of New World Negro societies was considered by Herskovits as a retention of the African ancestral cult. In Toco, Trinidad, for example, the ancestors exert considerable influence "in enforcing ethical and moral strictures, in aiding descendants when in difficulty, in sanctioning marriages, in keeping away evil magic and assuring safety in parturition" (Herskovits and Herskovits, 1947b, 300). In the same community, many aspects of the commemorative rites for the dead seem to be derived from Africa. Among these at the Toco wake are the following: "addressing the dead with candor, as though he were present, pouring water about the house, and in front of the coffin, the *bongo* dance and the story-telling and game-playing sessions . . ." (*ibid.*, 301). The "soul" concepts (soul, spirit, shadow, jumby) reflect Christian doctrine, but at the same time represent reinterpretations of the multiple-soul concept of West Africa and the Congo (*ibid.*, pp. 302–3). In Toco, the Negroes believe at death that the soul, the essence of the individual, returns to God. On the other hand, the "spirit" of a man becomes the ghost or jumby; it can be caught and its power used by a malevolent practitioner of magic. His shadow wanders while the person sleeps and may be summoned and "captured." If this happens, the victim becomes ill and can be cured by a dance given to induce the ancestors to free his spirit (*ibid.*).

In the baptisimal rites of the Catholic Church, Herskovits saw an important sanction taken over by the *vodun* religion in Haiti. Baptism was applied to all significant ceremonies: *loa* (gods) had to be baptized when they first took possession of a devotee, and the *humfort* (*vodun* temple), drums, rattle, and other ritual objects had to be sanctified in this manner (1937b, 271–72).

In his analysis of the spirit possession complex of Haitian *vodun* and other New World syncretistic cults, Herskovits developed more fully than others had done the significance of another series of

36

Africanisms (1937b, 269; 1941a, 216–19); Herskovits and Herskovits, 1947b, 309, 322–23, 334–35). In these reports and elsewhere, Herskovits discussed the behavior of possessed persons, the psychological release often associated with possession, the specific dances for specific deities, the use of iron to sound basic rhythms for the drums, the role of the rattle, and the counterclockwise direction in which the participants rotated. In the coastal area of Dutch Guiana,

> *The behavior of the drummers and singers who accompany the possessed dancers is almost identical with that witnessed in West Africa. The same relaxed movements of the fingers as the drummers sometimes even play rhythms identical with West African beats on the drumheads, the same swaying of the bodies by the singers that makes of their singing itself a dance, and the same cupped hands with which the clapping is done, all testify to the manner in which these descendants of Africa are but repeating motor habits current in the homeland of their ancestors. There is likewise little difference between the two regions—or, for that matter, between these two and what is found in the United States "shouting" churches—in the meaning of such a rite for the participants. Curing, the solution of practical difficulties, protection from the forces of evil operative here and now; the immediacy of the ends reflected in the words of songs and in the supplication to the gods might be the attitudes shown in prayers and sermons heard in Negro churches of this country. (1941a, 219)*

Herskovits gave some attention to the psychological side of possession in New World Negro religions and this aspect will be considered in chapter 7. In a discussion of the African heritage in the Caribbean, M. G. Smith (1957, 36) said that spirit possession is not found in all African societies; therefore, he argued that such possession in the Caribbean is not necessarily of African origin. Bourguignon (1970, 91) notes, however, that in a sample of 114 societies representative of sub-Saharan Africa, 82 percent exhibited institutionalized forms of dissociational states, 81 percent some kind of possession belief, and 66 percent possession trance.

37

In *vodun* and other Afro-Catholic syncretic cults, as in the Fon and Yoruba spirit cults in West Africa, initiation is not prompted by illness thought to be due to possession. This is not the case in the Ndoep cult of Senegal or the Zar cult of Ethiopia. This distinction is important because "the Fon-Yoruba group of cults were not marginal, therapeutic societies . . . but cults of worship, linked to the power structure and the establishment, whether of kinship and the state or of the kin group and the ancestors" (Bourguignon, 1970, 91). That no patterns of possession trance similar to those in *vodun* and related cults among other New World Negroes are known for European societies is significant. Demonic possession trance of earlier periods of European history was something to be feared, a pathological phenomenon which called for exorcism (*ibid.*, 91).

Simpson and Hammond (1957, 48–49) indicate the differences between spirit possession in many Caribbean cults and the seizures in possessions that occurred during the Scotch-Irish revival in Ulster in 1859 and in camp meetings in Kentucky in the nineteenth century. In the latter situations, the minister condemned the wickedness of his hearers and portrayed Hell in vivid terms. Listeners felt guilty and were afraid; they wept, shouted, prayed, fell on the ground, jerked, shook in every joint, barked like dogs, and burst out into a "holy laugh" (Davenport, 1905, 78–81).

Revivalist leaders in Jamaica and in the Shouters church of Trinidad do not frighten their followers into a state of possession. It is a mark of distinction to be possessed by a spirit, and one benefits from the messages received during this religious experience. Also, in the Kentucky and the Scotch-Irish cases, devotees were possessed only by the Holy Spirit or, in a few cases, by the Devil, while in the African cults of Haiti, Brazil, Cuba, and Trinidad the possessing spirits are old African gods. Although some of the motor behavior described by Davenport is similar to that seen in the revivalist and "shouting" churches of the Caribbean and the United States, the muscular movements, particularly of the neck, shoulder, and back, appear to be almost identical in West Africa, Haiti, Cuba, Brazil, Trinidad, and Jamaica (Simpson and Hammond, 1957, 48–49).

The origins of possession trance in the Shakers or Spiritual Baptist groups of St. Vincent may lie in the violent conversions and dramatic seizures of early Methodism (Bourguignon, 1970, 93). In St. Vincent, there are no Afro-Caribbean cults of the Shango type as there are in Trinidad, or of the Cumina variety found in Jamaica, to exert an influence on the Shakers (*ibid.*, 91). Explanations of such variations in Afroamerican customs in terms of local conditions add to the work accomplished by Herskovits and other earlier investigators.

An interesting case of remodeling an aspect of religion found in Dahomey, among the Yoruba and other tribal groups in Nigeria, and to some extent in Ghana, is the period of seclusion for new devotees. Although changes in form have occurred, the meaning of this practice for the novitiate is similar in a number of the Afroamerican cults in the New World. Without proper teaching concerning such important matters as possession by a god, it is as difficult for one to be a full-fledged member of a cult group in Haiti or Trinidad as it is in Africa (1941a, 217; see also selection 7).

In the realm of magic, syncretisms of European and African beliefs and practices are numerous. In Haiti, Herskovits found that the forces behind protective magic are mainly the *loa*, while those utilized in harmful magic are the powers "that control the souls of the dead and those creatures of evil whose powers come from Satan . . ." These primary sanctions for malevolent magic, however, have been buttressed by the teachings of magical tracts from medieval Europe (1937b, 265–66). In dealing with supernatural forces, the view is widespread among New World Negroes that any power or charm can be used for both evil and good purposes. For example, Europeanized individuals in West Africa, as well as participants in syncretistic cults in the New World, associate Legba or Eshu with the Devil. In this identification, the Devil is not the personification of evil, but is one who can be helpful as well as malign (Herskovits and Herskovits, 1947b, 312).

Divination is widely practiced in West Africa, but it is also a part of Euro-American culture. Among New World Negroes, divinatory practices represent a synthesis of African and European traditions. Divination plays an important part in the lives of Paramaribo Negroes (Herskovits and Herskovits, 1936, 55, and see selection 8), and the frequency with which the Tocoan (Trinidad) consults his lookman (diviner), far exceeds European practice (Herskovits and Herskovits, 1947b, 312). In Porto Alegre, Brazil, divination is performed by the cult-head. The throw of the *kpele* (a chain of shells or nuts corresponding to the Yoruba *opele*), or of cowrie shells, foretells the outcome of future plans and reveals the will and wisdom of the gods (1943c, 500).

Another series of syncretisms based on both European and African traditions consists of the beliefs about witches and vampires. Methods of discovering, holding, and punishing witches—particularly the sprinkling of salt and pepper in the discarded skin of a witch—have been reported from Nigeria, Dahomey, Ghana (the Ashanti), Surinam, Haiti, Jamaica, Barbados, and Trinidad (1941a, 258–60). In Surinam the word for vampire is *azeman*, a term which has the same meaning in Dahomey; in Fon, *aze* is a witch, *azema* a vampire; in Nigeria the Yoruba word for witch is *aje* and the Edo word is *aze* (Herskovits and Herskovits, 1936, 43).

In summary, many aspects of West African religious beliefs and practices, as well as traditions related to religion, have been retained by New World Negro populations. In some cases, Africanisms have been retained almost without change; in others, reinterpretation of African traditions has occurred through modifying form but retaining its essential inner meaning or through retaining the same form but modifying its meaning. Particularly in the areas of magic, divination and witchcraft, the syncretisms of African and European customs are numerous. Herskovits contributed substantially to the work of those who preceded him in the study of Afroamerican religions and related aspects of culture.

Conclusion. In the light of the separatism advocated, at least temporarily, by some of the leaders in the black power movement of the late 1960s and the early 1970s, as well as by rightists in the white group, Herskovits' examination, in 1937, of the political implications of the retention of Africanisms in the New World is pertinent today:

Disconcertingly enough, it is those holding opinions concerning the Negro who sense the opportunity to bolster their par-

40

ticular theses by reference to the fact that Africanisms have been retained in the New World. On the left, the point of view taken conceives the Negroes of the United States as a subject "nation," whose true freedom and full citizenship may come only after the establishment of an autonomous Black Republic in the South shall have permitted the fulfillment of the inherent genius of this peo-ple. What better theoretical base for such a problem could be found than in material which seems to show that American Negroes, under their skins, are but Africans whose suppressed racial tendencies will, when released, furnish the drive needed for working out their own destiny? At the same time, those on the extreme right, who urge social and economic segregation for the American Negro, also indicate their position by contemplating the Africanisms retained in American Negro life. Is this not evidence, they say, of the inability of the Negro to assimilate white culture to any workable degree, and should not Negroes therefore be encouraged to develop their own peculiar "racial" gifts—always, that is, within the bounds of the Negro's place?

Neither conclusion is in the least justified. To say that American and New World Negroes have retained certain African patterns of behavior and certain African aspects of belief within a varying range is not to suggest that in this country, for example, they have not assimilated American culture. They have, in fact, assimilated it to the degree that their opportunities have permitted. (1937b, 303–4)

In the separatist philosophy espoused by the more militant black nationalists, desegregation and integration for ghetto Negroes are regarded as impossibilities in the foreseeable future. Some say that they do not want to be assimilated into what they regard as a life-style of questionable value. These persons urge Blacks to reject the values of "mainstream America" and to accept what they consider to be the more satisfying values of the black world. Support for "black culture" in the United States bears some resemblance to the concept of Negritude, which was popular in the French-speaking countries of West Africa during the nationalist movements of the 1950s and 1960s. Difficult to define briefly, Negritude is both a reaffirmation of pride in the cultures of Africa and a reaction to white domination. It is an

41

attempt both to find a gratifying identity in the modern world and to formulate a rallying cry for use in national and international power struggles. Herskovits' perception of the significance of pre-American patterns preceded that of the black intellectual leadership. The most ardent black nationalists, however, often refer to *The Myth of the Negro Past*. In that work, Herskovits asserted that the West African, South American, and West Indian data must be taken into full account if true perspective on the values of Negro life in the United States was to be gained (1941a, xiii).

The concept of "soul" (see C. Keil, 1966, 167–81 on the meaning of this term), an important part of the idea of black culture, may or may not be associated with the political concept of black power. And black power may or may not include black separatism. The black culture–black power movement of the late 1960s and early 1970s in the United States includes such varied aspects as black caucuses in higher education, politics, and religion; black studies in educational institutions; black art; knowledge of and pride in black cultural heroes and in African and Afroamerican history and cultures; community control of schools; welfare rights organizations; and black capitalism. This movement is symbolized by dashikis, beads, Afro hairstyles, African names, African and Afroamerican art objects. In short, the contemporary reaction of many Negroes to American segregation and discrimination is that black is beautiful, honorable, and powerful. The strengths of the black sociocultural configuration are proclaimed, regardless of the origin or the age of the configuration's components.

IV AESTHETICS

Art and music were lifelong interests of Melville Herskovits, and aesthetic studies were always included in his field research.

Plastic and Graphic Arts. The art forms of Dahomey were of great interest to the Herskovitses. As they pointed out, before the conquest by the French in 1892, the wealth of the king in gold, silver, and brass figures and in cloths was displayed in Abomey, the capital of Dahomey. The walls of the compounds occupied by the king and the highest ranking persons were decorated in bas-reliefs. The most important temples to the *vodun* (gods) were located in Abomey, and the most elaborate religious ceremonies were held there. Priests asked the best carvers to produce objects for them and for the shrines of the deities. At the time of the Herskovitses' field work in 1931, wood carving still provided the main artistic outlet in Dahomey. Whereas brass, silver, and cloth work were luxuries, wood carving was an essential part of every household. Appliqué designs were used outside the religious realm as symbols of the status of the king and other persons of high rank, as indications of the achievements of the societies of a social character, and, in some instances, as art objects (1938b, vol. 2, chaps. 35–37; and see selections 1 and 2).[1] The Herskovitses pointed out that while the brass pieces in Dahomey represent an independent tradition, the appliqué clothwork is derived from the bas-reliefs found on the compound walls of persons of high rank and on the walls of temples devoted to the gods (Herskovits and Herskovits, 1934a, 76).

On the reasons why African art has been so widely accepted in Europe and America, Herskovits said that "the mask and the human or animal figure are familiar forms in the Euro-American convention. Such forms, even though of African origin wrought in a different stylistic tradition, yet fall within the category of pure art, in contrast to so many of the handicrafts of nonliterate folk, such as their painted pottery, or decorated basketry" (1946c, 45).

In the art of the Bush-Negroes of Surinam the Herskovitses found parallels to some of the art of West Africa, but they said that these people had evolved "an art form that, in many respects, may be considered to be a new one" (Herskovits and Herskovits, 1930, 25–37, 48–49). Price's recent field work (Price, 1970, 363–76) shows that Saramaka woodcarving "was still in its infancy in 1850 and effloresced only during the early years of the present century." The question of

---

[1] Other examples of African art that have no religious significance were cited by Herskovits in a 1945 lecture: the Ashanti gold weights, Yoruba house posts, Ibo secret society masks, the Cameroon pipe bowls, Congo puberty rites, and war society masks (1946c, 60).

whether formal similarities between Bush-Negro art and West African art represent retentions or are the results of "independent innovation and development within historically related and overlapping sets of aesthetic ideas" has not yet been answered (*ibid.*, 375).

Twenty years after his comment in *Dahomey: An Ancient West African Kingdom* that criteria of good and bad art existed in Dahomey, Herskovits elaborated on the appreciation of art among nonliterate societies (1959d, 47–66). In these societies, standards are not verbalized, but he saw the difference as one of degree, not of kind. When Herskovits had rejected a poorly carved piece and praised a better one in Surinam, an informant said: "This man wants carving, not lumber." Bush Negroes were found to differ "in depth of feeling for the pieces, and in reasoning that guided appreciation, much as among ourselves."

Herskovits returned also to another theme he had developed briefly in *Dahomey*, namely, that art is not exclusively ritualistic in smaller, more or less isolated societies. The association of art with aspects of life other than religion is evident on the Northwest Coast of North America, where clans have their standings validated by the carvings on totem poles, and where artistry is used extensively in making storage boxes, house decorations, and ceremonial blankets. Other instances of nonreligious aspects of culture closely associated with art include the adzes of Mangaia (Cook Islands) that designate social position, the paintings by Plains Indians on buffalo hide that helped the warrior to validate his status during ceremonial boasting, the Eskimo carvings of animals, and the brass figurines and appliqué cloths of Dahomey referred to in chapter 2. Because art has nonreligious as well as religious aspects, Herskovits questioned the frequent assertion that "the arts of nonliterate peoples in contact with Euroamerican cultures are things of the past" (1959d, 62–63).

In discussing the role of the individual artist in nonliterate societies, Herskovits said that artistic creativity in these societies had not been explored. Persons of artistic bent, he argued, were "not too different" from such persons in Euro-American societies (1959d, 50, 65). In every society, stylistic conventions set the limits within which graphic and plastic artists work. An appreciation of the role of perception in art has had important effects on the aesthetic judgment of "modern" artists and art critics. As an example of the point that even a monochrome photograph is a convention, "a translation of a three-dimensional subject into two dimensions, with color transmuted into shades of black and white," Herskovits reported that a Bush Negro woman "turned a photograph of her own son this way and that, in attempting to make sense out of the shadings of greys on the piece of paper she held. It was only when the details of the photograph were pointed out to her that she was able to perceive the subject" (*ibid.*, 56).

Literature. Herskovits' strong interest in oral literature culminated in 1958 in the publication, with Frances S. Herskovits, of *Dahomean Narrative*. There, the authors follow the Dahomeans' twofold classification of narratives—the *hwenoho* (myths) and *heho* (tales). A storyteller explained: "We in Dahomey say that tales [*heho*] tell of things which never existed and are inventions of people. History [*hwenoho*] is the true story, and the life of Dahomey is based on history. But one learns from the tale what one can" (Herskovits and Herskovits, 1958a, 16). The Herskovitses distinguish subgroupings within each category of narratives. The *hwenoho* are subdivided into myths about the deities and the peopling of the earth; clan myths dealing with the origins of clans and their adventures through history; explanations of ritual behavior, food taboos, and sanctions for the ancestral code; and verse sequences composed by professional versifiers to aid in memorizing genealogies. The *heho* are subdivided into divination stories; hunter stories; *enfant terrible* stories (twins, orphans, children-born-to-die [*abiku*], abnormally born [*tohosu*]); Yo stories (humorous tales); tales of women (love, intrigue, and betrayal); and explanatory or moralizing tales. In contrast to the *hwenho*, the *heho* allow the storyteller greater latitude in interpretation, but there are limits to this elaboration. Thus, "the literary gallery of protagonists, whether superhuman, human, or animal, comprises identifiable personality types of which the narrator is fully cognizant. The Dahomean thinks of them in just such terms, so

45

that each becomes a symbol. . . . 'This is about Hunter,' a teller will begin; or he will say, 'This is an orphan story'; or 'This is another about Yo,' naming the mythical character who stands for all that is gross in appetite, but differs from the sexually unsatisfied trickster-deity Legba . . ." (*ibid.*, 23). The Tales of Women, like the Explanatory and Moralizing Tales, deal with the themes of conflict and fulfillment in human experience. These tales tell of devoted wives, the faithlessness of women, the loyalty of the best friend, but also of the betrayal of friendship, sibling rivalry, jealously between parent and child, and jealousy between cowives (*ibid.*, 33–35). Anthropomorphized birds and animals constitute the characters in most of the Explanatory and Moralizing Tales, and in many cases a farce dramatizes prohibited actions.

In Dahomey, riddle telling precedes storytelling, arousing interest among adults and serving as memory training for children. Of special interest is the double entendre in the riddles included in the rites for the dead. As the dead are sent away from the world of the living, they must "savor all that gave them pleasure when alive" (Herskovits and Herskovits, 1958a, 55). Of greater significance is the proverb. Approving or critical comments on human behavior in everyday speech frequently include proverbs, and proverbs are used in arguments presented in the courts. According to the Herskovitses, "the proverb phrases the philosophy and poetry of the Dahomeans" (*ibid.*, 57). In verse making, the third form of Dahomean nonnarrative expression, words are grouped in "tonal, rhythmic, and repetitive patterns in songs and chants" (*ibid.*, 57–58). Professional versifiers originate new songs in praise of the ancestors of important families and of the deeds of persons of high rank. These songs, based on old verses and interspersed with proverbs, are fashioned by persons of good memory. Professionals of this type are distinguished from "the creative maker of verse" who has "a heart that understands much" (*ibid.*, 58). Most of the new songs, however, are not improvised by professionals. Dahomean versifying includes indirection, allusion, metaphor, and the terse aphorism, but the Dahomean also uses the simple, direct statement, as is seen in an invocation sung at a small ancestral ceremony:

When one has need of something
Let him ask it of his *vodun* [god].
Long life, Grandfather!
We kneel before you
To ask for long life.

The song then asks for "new wives; for children to be born to these wives; for strength to work the fields; a harvest to reward labor" (*ibid.*, 69–70).

Dahomean narrative forms reveal a system of values that stresses the importance of realism in all relationships, discretion in speech, diplomacy in relations with others, the power of the ancestors, respect for parents, wealth, power and mobility, friendship and love and their opposites, social conformity, giving all of the facts to the diviner, and certain personal qualities—intelligence, industry, and using what is at hand (Herskovits and Herskovits, 1958a, 72–81).

One of the most stimulating parts of the Herskovitses' analysis of Dahomean narrative concerns the theme of sibling rivalry and the Oedipus thesis. They point out that while Rank and certain other psychoanalysts emphasize the hostility of the son toward his father, they ignore the fears the father has of being displaced by his son and the hostility between brothers. Criticizing the stress on unidirectional parent-child hostilities in the Freudian hypothesis, the Herskovitses say that these hostilities are "an expression of the broader phenomenon of intergenerational competition." They hypothesize that the attitudes found in sibling rivalry during infancy are later projected by the father upon the offspring (Herskovits and Herskovits, 1958a, 94–95; see also further commentary on this question in chapter 7).

Conceding that there are no means of determining origins, the Herskovitses reject Jung's concepts of the collective unconscious and the archetype in favor of a universalizing of symbolic experiences. Universals are seen as the result of the play of man's fantasy as "his constants of experience have been projected, elaborated, exaggerated" to endow forces greater than himself with the powers and personalities contained in world mythologies (Herskovits and Herskovits,

1958a, 99–100). That man has not done this everywhere in the same manner is shown in the case of trickster tales, illustrated by the differences between the Winnebago trickster and Legba and Yo in Dahomey. Comparing this American Indian trickster with Legba, they find that

> *Legba is neither creator nor destroyer; that what he gives and takes away is far more often individual than cosmogonic; that while he dupes others, he is rarely duped himself. His activity, again, is calculated, highly conscious. His acts are rarely impulsive, but for the most part are directed toward the achievement of a well-defined end. He knows socially accepted values even when he behaves contrary to them; he is in no wise the source of them.* (Herskovits and Herskovits, 1958a, 100–101)

Without rejecting the relationship between the two, they deny that myth arises from ritual. They do not question the role of myth in sanctioning social norms and social organization, nor do they overlook the influence of cultural imperatives among the factors encouraging creativity. In short, *Dahomean Narrative* sets forth a pluralistic theory of myth, and among the numerous theories advanced to explain the universality and the similarities of myths, it presents one of the most impressive.

Other studies of African and Afroamerican folklore by Herskovits included Kru proverbs (Herskovits and Tagbwe, 1930), Bulu tales (1949), Trinidad proverbs (1945e), and with Frances Herskovits pidgin English tales from Nigeria (1931) and from Ashanti (1938).

In Surinam, both in town and in the bush, the Herskovitses found that the proverb was heard more often than riddle and story. As is the case in Africa, proverbs are used in every kind of situation. In the bush the ability to use proverbs skillfully makes a man the equivalent of the scholar in Europe or the United States. In the town, proverbs are utilized most frequently in disputes, either as threats or as revilement. Since supernatural power is attributed to "cussing" in Surinam, as among Negroes in other parts of the New World and in Africa, it is safer in a quarrel to fall back on a traditional formula than to risk becoming involved in accusations and recriminations. This does not mean, however,

> that there are not sayings to comment fatalistically, or jibingly, or wittingly, on human experience. . . . Human ingratitude is remarked upon, and the faithlessness of women; . . . foolish show of courage is deplored, and boastfulness is ridiculed; . . . caution is recommended, and discretion, but not timidity; and the point is made that no one is so powerful or exalted that there is not someone to meet him on his own terms; greed is criticized, but reckless generosity is enjoined; the importance of wisdom is cited, and the role of necessity stated. (Herskovits and Herskovits, 1936, 136)

Unlike many New World Negro cultures where the riddle is at least as important as the proverb, riddling is not used frequently in Surinam outside the wake. Tales play an important part in Surinam life, especially in the rites for the dead. All stories are called Anansi tales, after the spider Anansi, the Twi trickster-hero of Ghana. In the bush, tales are told to amuse the dead during the six or seven days before burial. In Paramaribo, stories are told during all wakes and on anniversary celebrations for the dead, but the most important storytelling session occurs on the eighth night after death. Storytelling not associated with honoring or entertaining the dead is used to indoctrinate children and for amusement during ordinary gatherings in the "yard," or on the plantation or in work camps. Acknowledging the appreciable European influence in Surinam tales, the Herskovites suggested that the African correspondences for human as well as animal stories called for a reinvestigation of the conclusion that New World Negro tales involving kings and princes, demons and changelings are derived largely from European influences (Herskovits and Herskovits, 1936, 139–41).

In Haiti, Herskovits found the well-known types of African animal tales and stories of human tricksters and magicians. The character who corresponds to Anansi is the shrewd Ti Malice, while his victim is the stupid Bouki. The use of the proverb is widespread in

Haiti and its roles are essentially the same as in Africa and in Surinam, namely, to give moral instruction to the young, to express oblique thoughts in a quarrel, to sound a warning, or to comment sarcastically on a social situation. An old proverb was often heard in Mirebalais: *"Zafaï mouton pas zafaï cabrit"* ("The affairs of the sheep are not the affairs of the goat"), a warning against gossip (1937b, 264–65). Some Haitian proverbs originated in Europe, but the majority are African. In Toco, Trinidad, the guile of the characters in African animal tales is sometimes alluded to in divining sessions, but the Anansi tales have been relegated to the place of children's stories. African riddles and proverbs are seldom heard in Toco. Riddling is confined mainly to children; even the elderly folk rarely used proverbs (1945a, 195; Herskovits and Herskovits, 1947b, 314–15).

In 1970, Abrahams pointed out that the one aspect (among the many in Negro folklore studies said by Herskovits in 1943 to need more study) that has been most neglected is a reexamination of materials for similarities and differences on a regional basis. Although comparative analyses have been carried out on religious practices, little has been done "with the material central to the study of expressive culture: tales, riddles, proverbs, modes of address and conversation, and so forth" (Abrahams, 1970, 163). Verbal activity among Negro adolescents in the United States is known as "playing the dozens" or "sounding"; in the West Indies it is called "rhyming." Impromptu verbal contests are common among adults in ghettos of the United States and in rum shops, buses, and elsewhere in the West Indies. But there are also highly structured situations where the good talker can exhibit his talents. In the West Indies, the verbal virtuoso may limit himself to preaching, but frequently he performs in festivals, such as Carnival or Christmas, or at wakes or wedding celebrations.

Taking this pattern of performance, which involves the effective use of words, Abrahams compares three West Indian islands: Trinidad, Tobago, and Nevis. The man-of-words performance pattern in the Carnival *mas'es* (touring groups of masqueraders) is similar in Trinidad and Tobago, except that in Tobago one type of troupe, *Speech Band*, places less emphasis on the virtuoso and gives the

50

younger men a chance to speak. Hence, a war-of-words in *Speech Mas'* in Tobago is a team affair. Abrahams found that Nevis folklore is predominantly British in terms of the actual items performed, but "in terms of the context, the way in which a performance is organized, Nevis traditional expression is a development of the man-of-words pattern with its many African antecedents and analogues" (Abrahams, 1970, 171). Whereas in Tobago there was always a balance between the virtuoso and the integrated patterns of performance, with a drift in recent years toward a sense of community enterprise, the emphasis in Nevis is on solo performance and there is little community activity or feeling. This study shows that non-aesthetic forces may affect aesthetic activities and that the man-of-words performances "represent a model of interpersonal relations in the surrounding community" (*ibid.*, 176).

Music and the Dance. Herskovits' strong concern about music resulted in important contributions to ethnomusicology. He set forth some basic principles for the study of African music, and emphasized the value of music in Afroamerican studies. His recordings of singing and instrumental music in Surinam, Dahomey, Ashanti, Nigeria, Togoland, Trinidad, and Brazil are of great significance to ethnomusicologists. All of his studies of musical form had a historical dimension and were related to the cultural contexts within which they existed (Merriam, 1964, 89–90).

In 1929, the Herskovitses recorded 255 songs from the Bush Negroes living in settlements along the Surinam River, and from persons of African descent in Paramaribo, the principal city of Surinam. These songs, transcribed and analyzed by M. Kolinski, a musicologist, were published in 1936 (Herskovits and Herskovits, 1936, 491–515). Except for a few songs, Bush Negro music was found to be essentially African. Among the coastal Negroes, music showed a strong European influence, but 23 percent of their songs were of African type (*ibid.*, 517). A number of problems arose in recording these songs. Subjects were willing to sing songs into the phonograph for the pleasure of hearing them reproduced immediately thereafter, but they were in many cases unwilling to give the texts

51

of the songs they had sung. In such instances, it was necessary to replay the songs to residents of other villages in order to verify the names of the songs, and to play them again for explanations. For several reasons, informants were reluctant to give texts: revealing what another had attempted to distort involved spiritual danger; there existed an edict of the ancestors that no man might reveal more than half of what he knew; replaying songs that name important gods or ancestors was considered dangerous. Because of these resistances, many of the texts had to be worked out by replaying the songs after the field work had been completed (*ibid.*, 525-26).

During their field work in West Africa in 1931, the Herskovitses recorded 464 melodies, mainly from Dahomey and the Ashanti of Ghana; but they also included a few Yoruba songs from Nigeria and the coastal region of Togoland. Herskovits' discussion of Dahomean music is ethnological (1938b, 2:317). The technical analysis of the Dahomean scales and manner of singing was done by Kolinski.

In Dahomey, vocal music is predominant. Aside from the zither, ivory trumpets, and reed flutes, Dahomeans employ only such percussion instruments as the gong, the rattle, and most importantly the drum. In pre-conquest days, the trumpets were used with drums to announce the presence of royalty, but for decades they have been used rarely. Herskovits emphasized that all the instruments "are commonly merely accessory to the songs which they accompany" (1938b, 2:320). A basic beat must be set and maintained for all types of Dahomean music. Among the types of songs recorded in Dahomey by the Herskovitses are religious songs for the glorification of the gods of every pantheon; praise songs for the royalty of earlier days and for contemporary chiefs; funeral songs; songs of "allusion" sung to taunt an enemy or rivals; songs sung at social dances; *dokpwe* (cooperative work group) songs; the songs of weavers, hunters, cloth-workers, and ironworkers; lullabies; songs of praise for a best friend; and songs sung by various mutual-aid associations in praise of their own deeds. Other songs serve as carriers of history in reporting the ritual connected with the giving of offerings to the souls of those taken into slavery (*ibid.*, 321).

In his analysis of Dahomean singing, Herskovits gave attention to the forms of songs, their duration, and the musical treatment of them. Songs glorifying the deeds of former kings and living chiefs were preceded by prolonged rehearsals. Choruses made up of the younger wives of a chief consisted of from fifteen to forty women under the direction of a woman who conducted in a manner similar to that of a European choirmaster. The songs had many stanzas, and the words were characterized by extravagant metaphor (1938b, 321–22). In contrast, the songs accompanying dances in the market-places or some of the songs sung in ancestral and Sagbata (Daho-mean Earth deity) ceremonies were improvisations. Here the music was less complex, the rhythms more regular, and the melodies simpler. In these songs, there was a notable lack of association be-tween words and music; the opposite was true of the songs sung by the choruses of chiefs' wives (*ibid.*). Except for the a cappella singing by trained choruses of women, the pattern of musical ex-pression was mainly that of leader-and-chorus alternation, "the phrases being short and the number of repetitions of a given phrase considerable" (1946c, 41). Herskovits found that music, the dance, and versification were intertwined in Dahomey. Dancing was the "supreme expression of worship" but it was also an outstanding form of recreation. The choreography in ritual dances was elaborate; in social dances, greater freedom of expression was permitted (*ibid.*).

In the New World, the attitudes of the masters toward song, dance, and folktale varied from hostility to encouragement. In some cases trivial matters such as the volume of noise made in singing or dancing affected white attitudes. When African types of singing and dancing did not interfere with work or were performed on holidays, white onlookers enjoyed them as much as the participating slaves. Because tales were told quietly, this aspect of African culture was widely retained (1941a, 138).

The virtuosity attained by dancers and drummers in Haitian reli-gious gatherings is not exceeded among other Caribbean Negro cul-tures or in Africa. Here the musical forms consist mainly of African rhythms, but the melodic line varies from unchanged European folk songs to purely African songs. "In the use of the falsetto, however, in the statement of a theme by a leader and its repetition by a chorus,

53

and in the countless modulations introduced into the song, the singing is entirely African as are the postures struck by those singing" (1937b, 263). The 300 songs recorded by Herskovits in Haiti, like those he recorded in Surinam and Dahomey, were analyzed by Kolinski.

In 1941–1942, the Herskovitses recorded religious music in Bahia, Brazil, as part of the program in the Archive of American Folk Song in the Music Division of the Library of Congress. In Bahia, as in other Afroamerican and West African groups, rhythm is highly important in music. In addition to the use of drums, rhythm is marked in religious settings by handclapping, striking a pottery jar with a fire-fan, and beating a calabash with sticks. In the public rituals, drummers play the rhythms that call the deities, induce possession, control the dance patterns, and occasionally represent the voice of the god who has been summoned. The technique of drumming is handed down from father to son, and having drummers of repute in the family is a source of pride. Because of their knowledge about the gods and their mastery of the rhythms to accompany songs in honor of each god of each "nation," a strong feeling of identity exists within a drummers' group (1944b, 477–92). According to the Herskovitses, Afro-Bahian cult music should be regarded as polyrhythmic rather than polyphonic. Percussion is so important that singing is an accompaniment to the drumming rather than the opposite, as is the case in Euro-american music. Drums and iron gongs are used for the West African and Congo-Angola ceremonies, while Caboclo (Indian) groups mark the rhythms with a large calabash and a rattle (Herskovits and Herskovits, 1947a, 1–15). Voice quality has little to do with good singing; a good song leader is a person who can designate the proper song for any god of any "nation" who may be summoned or who may appear. Herskovits collaborated with Waterman on a technical analysis of Afro-Bahian cult songs (Herskovits and Waterman, 1949).

In 1939, Herskovits reported the preliminary results of a musicological comparison by Kolinski between African and American Negro music. In this study of African traits in American spirituals,

Thirty-six were found to have the same scales (tonal structures) as specific songs in the West African collection, while identical correspondences in melodic line were even found in a few instances. Thirty-four spirituals had the same rhythmic structure as some of the West African melodies, while the formal structure of fifty spirituals—their phrasing and time—were found to have African counterparts. (1941a, 268)

Herskovits warned that knowledge of the ways in which the African musical idiom was combined with the European to produce these songs would require continual analysis of factual materials (1939, 31–32).

In Trinidad, the Herskovitses found that a large collection of songs showed that "there is, on the whole, more of Africa than of Europe in the music" (Herskovits and Herskovits, 1947b, 316). African characteristics included the emphasis on rhythm, the tendency to introduce polyrhythms, the antiphony between leader and chorus in singing, and the use of intervals typical of African music. The calypso, the most popular of Trinidad song types, uses song to comment critically on current events, a pattern that is widespread in West Africa. Some of the tunes are modifications of European folk music; the words are in English, but the pattern of sarcastic improvisation is African (*ibid.*, 317).

In view of Herskovits' studies of New World Negro music over a period of more than thirty years, one of the principal findings of Lomax's recent investigation is of considerable interest: "Afro-American music, considered as a whole, is a sub-system of a continental Black African style tradition that seems to be one of the most ancient, consistent, and fertile of world musical families" (Lomax, 1970, 181). Lomax's study of world song style "strongly confirms the position taken by Herskovits in *Myth of the Negro Past* (1958, 262–267)" (*ibid.*, 197).

Language. At a time when very few scholars were concerned with the languages spoken by New World Negroes, Herskovits pointed out that if each West African tribe were linguistically independent, communication among the slaves would have been extremely difficult. On the other hand, if the differences were mainly in vocabulary rather than in construction, mutual understanding would have occurred in a relatively short time (1941a, 80–81).

Comparing linguistic traits in the texts they recorded in Surinam in 1929 with those of the Sudanic languages of West Africa, Herskovits concluded that

> the Negroes who reached the New World acquired as much of the vocabulary of their masters as they initially needed or was later taught to them, pronounced the words as best they were able, but organized them into their aboriginal speech patterns. Thus arose the various forms of Negro-English, Negro-French, Negro-Spanish, and Negro-Portuguese spoken in the New World, their "peculiarities" being due to the fact that they comprise European words cast into an African grammatical mold. But this emphatically does not imply that these dialects are without grammar, or that they represent an inability to master the foreign tongue, as is so often claimed. (1941a, 280)

In 1964, Dillard, a linguist who specializes in the study of Afroamerican creole languages, said that "it is remarkable how well Herskovits' statements, considered in their general tenor, stand up against the works of specialists in linguistics. . . . A section of *Suriname* [sic] *Folk-lore* may prove to be the most valuable thing ever written on the languages of the Caribbean" (Dillard, 1964, 36–41).

Herskovits cited the work of Turner on the speech of Sea Island Negroes in the 1930s as standing almost alone at that time. Turner had found approximately four thousand West African words in the vocabulary of the Negroes in coastal South Carolina and Georgia, as well as "many survivals in syntax, inflections, sounds, and intonation" (personal communication from Turner to Herskovits, 1941a, 276, 323). In Georgia he had recorded several songs that were wholly African, as well as some songs and tales that contained both African

56

and English words. Turner also discovered many compound words made up of African and English parts and many African given names. In some cases, "whole African phrases appear in Gullah without change either of meaning or pronunciation" (*ibid.*, 276).

A number of new languages—Sranan (Negro English of Surinam), Saramakkan, Papiamentu, Negro Dutch in Surinam, and several forms of French Creole in the Caribbean and in Louisiana have developed during the past three centuries (Taylor, 1960, 277–88; reprinted in Horowitz, 1971, 77–91). According to Taylor, at first the "pidgins" (*lingua franca*) were used only between Africans and Europeans, and between Africans of different tribal backgrounds. Later, the pidgins became "creolized"—adopted as the languages of whole communities—and evolved as other idioms do according to their native speakers' changing needs of communication (Taylor in Horowitz, 78–79). Taylor's conclusion is the same as Herskovits', namely, that these languages "are peculiar in combining rather similar grammatical structures of a non-Indo-European and seemingly West African type with vocabularies that are predominantly of English, Portuguese or Spanish, Dutch and French ancestries . . ." (*ibid.*, 78). Although little is known about the history of creolized languages, it is known that the early French settlers and missionaries used a *petit-nègre* to communicate with the slaves. Probably this jargon became a model that was modified by the Africans, and, in turn, was adapted by the Whites, who tried to Gallicize the vocabulary (*ibid.*, 78–79).

Codes of polite behavior among New World Negroes reflect African traditions. Components of this behavior are seen in the respect shown elderly persons and in turning the head when laughing. Another reworking of African polite behavior is the discourse between preacher and congregation in which such expressions as "Yes, Lord" are interspersed with the words of the sermon. This pattern of behavior has been observed in Surinam, the West Indies, and the United States. In the Caribbean, passive listening to the words of another in an ordinary encounter is regarded as rudeness (1941a, 152–53). Likewise, diplomacy and reserve represent the continuation of West African tradition. The survival value of discretion during and

57

after slavery reinforced the principle of indirection, but traditional sanctions underlie this behavior (*ibid.*, 158). Reisman's analysis of the way cultural symbols are handled in Antigua through "masking," "reinterpretation," and "remodeling" deals with "fundamental value patterns first extensively noted by Herskovits"—reticence and discretion, respect and acceptance rather than confrontation—norms that are closely related to an indirect and ambiguous mode of expression (Reisman, 1970, 129–44).

Art and Acculturation. An understanding of Afroamerican art requires a knowledge of West African art and of the contacts which Africans and their descendants have had with Europeans in the New World. Where the ratio of slaves to Whites was high, African cultural traits were retained to a greater degree than where the proportion was small. The European influence on Afroamerican culture varied with the colonial status of each territory—Portuguese, Spanish, French, English, or Dutch—and the kind of adjustment that persons of African descent were forced to make. Since this adjustment was greater for those in the upper social strata, Afroamerican art, as a rule, does not come from these levels. Verbal, musical, and choreographic forms of art can be performed regardless of restrictions on the personal freedoms of a people, but the graphic and plastic arts require special training and an opportunity to practice them. While some wood carving was used in religious rituals in Bahia and in Rio Grande, Brazil, as late as the end of the nineteenth century, and paintings are found on the walls of *vodun* cult centers in Haiti, work in the plastic and graphic arts along West African lines is almost altogether absent in the New World (1959b, 150–58).

In his studies of aesthetics in a situation where the representatives of two cultures are in continuous contact, Herskovits noted the degree to which "cultural imponderables"—the elements of a culture that are "carried below the level of consciousness"—are retained. Among those he listed are linguistic patterns, musical style, and sanctions for types of motor habits, systems of values, and codes of etiquette (1945c, 5–24). His research indicated that "those elements in culture that intrude but slightly upon consciousness are taken for granted, and are thus far more difficult to dislodge from the thought and behavior patterns of individuals subjected to a new culture than those which must be given continuous attention" (*ibid.*). Earlier we cited some of the evidence on this point in discussing the persistence of African grammatical configurations, African rhythms, such motor habits as dancing and method of planting, indirect modes of behavior, and systems of values which are a part of non-European ritual and theology and of family traditions.

V   ECONOMIC ANTHROPOLOGY

Melville Herskovits' interest in economics resulted in the publication of *The Economic Life of Primitive Peoples* (1940), the first general text in that field, and in a revision of this work, *Economic Anthropology: A Study in Comparative Economics* (1952). In these writings, Herskovits criticized the early principle of economic theory that the individual is the starting point for all development of theoretical principles. He argued that "social interaction in terms of cultural tradition" required reconsideration of the earlier assumption. He agreed that ". . . man's economy, as a rule, is submerged in his social relationships" but he questioned Polanyi's assertion that a member of a nonliterate society "does not act so as to safeguard his individual interest in the possession of material goods; he acts so as to safeguard his social standing, his social claims, his social assets" (1952a, 7; Polanyi, 1944, 46). In Herskovits' view, Economic Man should not be rejected only to be replaced by Society as a method of explaining economic behavior. To understand such behavior, he added the role of individual choice to the resources of the society and the values of the culture (1952a, 8).

Herskovits admitted that the entrepreneurial function, if it is present at all, is minimal in nonliterate, nonmachine societies. Also, in these societies, the profit motive is not a major characteristic of production and distribution, and labor is not usually for hire (1952a, 10–11). In one sense, Herskovits said, the difference between the distributive systems in the simplest economies and the industrialized societies is one of kind. In the simplest economies, the pecuniary factor is absent; "what elementary types of exchanges of goods and

59

services occur are on the basis of an immediate, *ad hoc* kind of give and take. . . . The market is present in such rudimentary form that it exists by definition only . . ." (*ibid.,* 14). Unlike some students of economic anthropology, however, Herskovits did not lose sight of "intermediate societies" such as those in Central America or West Africa.

In these more complex systems, where the market, distinguishable as such in its institutionalized forms, and based on exchanges involving the use of pecuniary media—money—is present, the complexity of the process that marks the movement of goods and services to the ultimate consumer in industrial communities is almost entirely lacking. This derives from the fact that even among nonliterate peoples, whose economies are of this order of complexity, the individual controls a substantial proportion of the techniques employed by his group in the basic tasks of getting a living, in addition to whatever specialized skills he may possess in the production of capital and consumption goods. . . . As far as the necessities of life are concerned, distribution is in large measure a process of allocating what has been produced by members of the household to those who constitute its personnel. Such commercial transactions as do take place, except among social aggregates large enough to permit a degree of specialization rare in nonliterate societies, are again personal, direct, and specific. . . . To the extent that the market in such societies does possess an objective and formal existence, it is a mechanism that facilitates the exchange of goods between members of different communities rather than between those who belong to the same group. (1952a, 14–15)

Herskovits found some similiarities in the economic life of all types of societies. First, dissimilarities in the scarcity of goods in the face of the wants of different peoples are, he thought, a matter of degree rather than of kind (1952a, 17–18). Second, he held that cross-culturally, the individual tends to maximize his satisfactions in terms of the choices he makes. This point was qualified by the statement that in societies other than those in Europe and America, "rational" means that the deferment of wants is disadvantageous, and there is no tradition of expanding production and increasing services (*ibid.*, 24). Third, the members of all societies devise implements to increase their technological competence, develop systems of exchange and patterns of consumption, and establish standards of value that affect choices among the alternatives available in the productive and distributive processes (*ibid.*, 487).

Although Herskovits indicated the similarities in our own and other economies, he was careful to add that comparisons should always include consideration of the effects of machine technology, pecuniary media, and the elaboration of business enterprise (1952a, 487). Finally, on the question of "communism" versus "individualism" in "primitive" societies, he pointed out that though "the principle of mutual aid is widespread among nonliterate folk, it is by no means universal or exists to the exclusion of competition based on individualistic striving for economic goals" (*ibid.*, 499–500).

In sum, as Vaughan says, Herskovits "stressed the importance of the cultural context of economic behavior," but "he adopted the conventional 'formal' definition of economics, the application of scarce means to given ends, and in the main, tried to follow the categories of academic economics in ordering his data" (Vaughan, 1968, 354).

In 1941, Frank H. Knight published a critique of *The Economic Life of Primitive Peoples* (reprinted in Herskovits, 1952a, 507–23). Knight argued that economic theory is the one social science "which effectively uses inference from clear and statable abstract principles, and especially intuitive knowledge, as a method. . . . All other social sciences are empirical . . ." (*ibid.*, 511). Knight urged anthropologists to grasp the difference between economics as an exposition of principles and as a descriptive exposition of facts (*ibid.*, 516). For the economist, Knight thought that a knowledge of scientific anthropology might have the same kind of "broadening" effect as actual travel and a wide range of reading in history and all branches of literature. As Knight envisioned economic theory, "authentic" facts

61

about economies other than our own "are not necessarily more useful than travelers' tales based on superficial and largely false impressions" (*ibid.*, 517).

Knight criticized Herskovits' use of such concepts as production, wealth, capital, money, and "economic surplus" (1952a, 515). He claimed that Herskovits treated "all interests and activities above the animal level as wasteful and as expressing an immoral struggle for domination and display" (*ibid.*, 521). In the following paragraph, Knight acknowledged that "a writer of intelligence could hardly be so blinded by a theoretical prepossession as to be quite as consistently wrong as we have indicated." He then quotes Herskovits' statement: "Nor is it intended to suggest that members of the leisure class [two groups, those who govern and those who command techniques for placating and manipulating the supernatural forces of the universe] occupy their time purposelessly, or that they are not often hard-driven by the cares and preoccupations of their obligations towards the groups from which they derive their support." Nevertheless, Knight thought he was justified in saying that "politics and religion, as well as art and recreation are practically viewed in Veblenian terms, as nonutilitarian and 'invidious' activities" (*ibid.*, 521).

In his rejoinder, Herskovits said that the establishment of the study of comparative economics would be difficult if the deductive view held by Knight came to be widely accepted. It seemed to him that no social science could "accomplish its ends if it disregards the first commandment of science in general—that only through constant and continuing cross-reference between hypothesis and fact can any understanding of problems and valid interpretations of data be had" (1952a, 524). He asked whether Professor Knight would consider it advisable to use a fiction to illustrate a point, when the point could be illustrated by referring to what actual social groups really do in the productive and distributive process. He considered the description of "man" given by Knight—"a competitive, contentious, and combative animal, given to self-aggrandizement and inclined to make this end justify nearly any means" as inadequate in the light of data from many societies on the wide range of human personalities (*ibid.*, 526). Calling attention to his critic's comments on schools of economic thought which differed from Knight's own point of view, Herskovits added that not all economists found his discussion of comparative economics as uncongenial as did Knight (*ibid.*, 528). Herskovits reiterated his point that economic "laws" based on a single culture, even a complex one, are "equivalent to a statistical average based on a single case." In Herskovits' view, "if there are those 'universal principles of economy' that, according to Professor Knight, are 'the beginning of any logical approach to the problems' of economics, then they must be verified by study of the actual facts concerning the economic life of as many different societies as can be reached" (*ibid.*, 529). It was Herskovits' hope that the disciplines of anthropology and economics could join "in contributing to a deeper understanding of the range of variation in man's method of getting a living, and in documenting any general principles to be drawn from such facts, which will help us the better to understand our own economic institutions and behavior" (*ibid.*, 531). In such matters as the importance of specialization of labor, the significance of gift exchange, the role of prestige, and the nature of property, he thought that anthropologists could contribute effectively to economics. On the other hand, he thought that anthropologists would benefit from a knowledge of the conceptual and methodological tools and the range of problems of economists.

Polanyi (Polanyi *et al.*, 1957) was more skeptical than Herskovits about the application of traditional economics to nonliterate societies, and some of Polanyi's followers went further than he did. Dalton, a Northwestern University economist, emphasizes the distinction between the substantive meaning of economic ("the provision of material goods which satisfy biological and social wants") and the economizing meaning of economic ("a special set of rules designed to maximize the achievement of some end or to minimize the expenditure of some means"). He argues that "primitive" economy differs from market industrialism not in degree but in kind (Dalton, 1961, 20). In his view, "The absence of machine technology, pervasive market organization, and all-purpose money, plus the fact that economic transactions cannot be understood apart from social obligation, create . . . a non-Euclidean universe to which Western economic theory cannot be fruitfully applied" (*ibid.*, 20). In the Western meaning of the term, Dalton says, "there is no 'economy' in primitive society, only socio-economic institutions and processes" (*ibid.*, 21).[1] In a critique of Dalton's paper, LeClair argues that "the postulates of scarcity and economizing calculation are of universal relevance" (LeClair, 1962, 1184). LeClair advocates a functional approach in the study of economic systems: the product mix, or what goods are to be produced and in what quantities; the problem of factor proportions, or the relative proportions of land, labor, and capital to be used in producing goods; and the distribution of product (*ibid.*, 1190). LeClair accepts Dalton's opposition to the uncritical application of economic concepts to "apparently similar phenomena in 'primitive' societies," but he hopes to avoid abandoning "everything which is potentially fruitful in contemporary economic thought" (*ibid.*, 1196).

Paul Bohannan emphasizes the differences between industrial and nonindustrial economies: the principle of contract, market exchange, the measurement of the factors of production (land, work, ingenuity, and capital) by a single or general-purpose money, and the presence of machines (Bohannan, 1963, 218–19). Bohannan traces the shift in economic theory from "value" to "price," and utilizes Polanyi's three modes of allocation (reciprocity, redistribution, and market exchange) in his analysis of the economic integration of society. A "subsistence economy" is defined as one in which "the factors of production are not transacted by the market mechanism" (*ibid.*, 241). In West Africa, for example, the market has been peripheral in the past, but in recent years it has been gaining in importance (*ibid.*, 241–44).

After the publication of the revised version of his text on economic anthropology in 1952, Herskovits commented from time to time on concepts and findings in this field. In the Preface to *Markets in*

[1] In 1971, Dalton regarded economic anthropology "as having two principal empirical foci: modernization and the study of the economies of traditional bands, tribes and peasantries" as they were organized before European colonial presence, enlarged commercialization, and the beginnings of industrialism began to change them (Dalton, 1971a; 1971b, 23–24).

Africa, edited by Bohannan and Dalton, he admitted that it is not easy to see similarities between rudimentary economies and the great industrial complexes. Although the economic nature of some modes of exchange may be distorted by ritual demands or kinship rules, he held that shifting from the classification of form to analysis of function results in no more than extremes of a continuum. In his view:

> If a given economic—or social, or political, or religious—institution is unique to the culture in which it is found, and we go no further than this, refusing to utilize any common nomenclature, classification and concepts will be ruled out, and the question arises as to the possibility of ever drawing comparisons. But without recourse to the method of comparison, we are left with no more than a series of discrete descriptions, from which generalizations cannot be drawn. This is why we must search for the functional unities that underlie the formal differences. (Bohannan and Dalton, 1962, xvi)

This approach would mean, for example, putting aside the formal aspects of markets and looking at the common factor of exchange. Consideration would be given to the role of local markets as well as to the patterns of the world economic system. Saying that credit is not limited to price-profit systems, Herskovits pointed out that in the aboriginal economies of West Africa, the pawn was collateral for a loan. Also, reinsurance, or risk distribution, is implicit in the decentralization of herds in East Africa (*ibid.*, xiv–xv).

There was, then, a long, more or less underground conflict between Herskovits and his students—LeClair and Schneider on the one hand and Daltan and Bohannan on the other—about all of the major issues in economic anthropology. To some extent, *Markets in Africa*, edited by Bohannan and Dalton, is an attempt to refute Herskovits' position, and Dalton continued the controversy in the correspondence section of the *American Anthropologist* during the middle and late 1960s. Their differing viewpoints in this field constituted a major point in the deep disagreements between Herskovits and Bohannan, the anthropologist selected by the Northwestern administration for a major position in the Department of Anthropology and in the Program of African Studies.

In 1958, Herskovits presented some of the economic aspects of the African-derived candomble cult-group in Bahia. The volume of retail trade devoted to cult paraphernalia in the established markets of that city is impressive, and commodities imported from Africa are of some importance (1958a, 248–49). A considerable part of the food that is vended on the streets is sold by cult-initiates, and the foods are African (*ibid.*, 250). Moreover, candomble women comprise a large segment of the market vendors. These women deal in all kinds of commodities and, like West African women traders, are known for their business acumen. Other candomble women work as nursemaids, cooks, seamstresses, shop girls—tasks usually performed by Brazilian urban women (*ibid.*, 252). Male cult-affiliates may be found throughout the occupational scale, but with the highest concentration in its lower levels.

Another phase of candomble economics is found in the offerings a member makes to the deities for favors received and the fees he pays to priests or priestesses who intervene for him (*ibid.*, 253–54). Herskovits indicated that the amounts required for active participation in the cults were considerable, and that the entire incomes of the most renowned priests came from their professional work. In some cases, a cult-group came to be regarded as a cooperative unit, and it was difficult to separate the income of the group from that of its head. In such groups, some initiates lived at the centers, members might receive loans from the "gods," and pressure might be exerted on devotees to increase their earnings and thus enhance the resources of the candomble as an economic unit (*ibid.*, 263).

Herskovits' last commentary on comparative economics stressed the inadequacy of traditional economics when applied to economies in the process of rapid change. Students of economic growth, he said, have to account for observed differences in developing societies and to explain these differences in the light of the general principles of economics (Herskovits and Harwitz, eds., 1964, 5). For the study of the new economic settings, Herskovits favored modifying the conventional concepts and principles rather than abandoning them and starting anew.

In this brief examination of economic anthropology, we have endeavored to show how Melville Herskovits contributed to the development of comparative economics, both through his texts and other writings in this field, and through the influence he has exerted on other scholars interested in nonindustrial economies and economies that are being increasingly influenced by industrial development. Due to the work of Herskovits, Knight, Firth, Polanyi, Dalton, Bohannan, Schneider, LeClair, and others, the relationships between economics and anthropology have been discussed more or less continuously during the past thirty years.[2]

VI PHYSICAL ANTHROPOLOGY

One of Herskovits' earliest scientific interests centered in physical anthropology, specifically in a program titled "Variability under Radical Crossing." These studies dealt with variability, homogeneity and heterogeneity, and the problem of Mendelian inheritance in race crossing (Merriam, 1964, 83–84).[1] This research culminated

[2] See C. S. Belshaw, *Traditional Exchange and Modern Markets* (Englewood Cliffs, N.J.: Prentice-Hall, 1965); Robbins Burling, "Maximization Theories and the Study of Economic Anthropology," *American Anthropologist* 64 (1962): 802–21; Scott Cook, "The Obsolete 'Anti-Market' Mentality: A Critique of the Substantive Approach to Economic Anthropology," *American Anthropologist* 68 (1966): 323–45; Raymond Firth, *Primitive Polynesian Economy* (London: Routledge, 1939); Clifford Geertz, *Peddlers and Princes* (Chicago: University of Chicago Press, 1963); Bert F. Hoselitz, *Sociological Aspects of Economic Growth* (Glencoe, Ill: The Free Press, 1960); Andrew M. Kamarck, "Economics and Economic Development," in *The African World*, ed. Robert A. Lystad (New York: Praeger, 1965), pp. 221–41; E. E. LeClair and H. S. Schneider, *Economic Anthropology* (New York: Holt, Rinehart & Winston, 1968); W. A. Lewis, *The Theory of Economic Growth* (London: George, Allen & Unwin, 1954); Manning Nash, *Primitive and Peasant Economic Systems* (San Francisco: Chandler, 1966); Walter C. Neale, "On Defining 'Labor' and 'Services' for Comparative Studies," *American Anthropologist* 66 (1964): 1300–1307; and Eric Wolf, *Anthropology* (New York: Prentice-Hall, 1964).

[1] Titles in physical anthropology by Herskovits other than those referred to in this section are given in Merriam's article and in the "Bibliography of Melville J. Herskovits," by Anne Moneypenny and Barrie Thorne (1964, 91 ff.). The following publications are especially noteworthy: "Age Changes in Pigmentation of American Negroes," *American Journal of Physical Anthropology* (1926a): 321–27; "Anthropometry," *Encyclopedia of the Social Sciences* 2 (1930a): 110–12; "Domestication," *ibid.*, 5 (1931): 206–8; "Race Mixture," *ibid.* 13 (1934b): 41–43; "Physical Types of West African Negroes," *Human Biology* 9 (1937c): 483–97.

Melville J. Herskovits

in two major publications, *The American Negro: A Study in Racial Crossing* (1928) and *The Anthropometry of the American Negro* (1930b).

When Herskovits stated in 1928 that the American Negro population had undergone extensive crossing, his view was a minority one. One example of this divergence was the United States Census of 1920. According to that report, 84.1 percent of the U.S. Negro population was "Black"—that is, of unmixed African ancestry, or in the language of the report, "Negroes of full blood." The 1920 Census found that 15.9 percent of the Negro population was "mixed." Since the Census of 1910 had reported the proportion of "Mulattoes" as 20.9 percent, the 1920 returns were rather puzzling. Less cautious scholars accepted the reliability of the 1920 figures, usually claiming that the great majority of Negroes in the "Black Belt" were unmixed Africans, but that those in the North were considerably mixed. Herskovits pointed out that some writers, including Jerome Dowd (1926), dichotomized the Negro population into a small, discontented and militant Mulatto group and a large, sluggish, more or less irresponsible unmixed black group.

The Herskovits study was primarily an anthropometric one, based on the measurement of certain physical traits; but this method was supplemented by genealogical reports. Since it was widely believed in the 1920s that 80 to 85 percent of the American Negro population was of unmixed African descent, Herskovits' finding of 22 percent was startling. Another conclusion of importance was the proportion of Negroes in the sample (27.3 percent) who claimed to have some American Indian ancestry (1928, 9–10).

Herskovits also examined race mixture in the United States from the point of view of the variability of American Negroes. His conclusion that the American Negro represents a definite physical type was based on the fact that, in his samples, the variability in selected physical characteristics is no greater than that found among any of the so-called "pure races" (African, European, and American Indian) from which they have come (1928, 49). Two lines of reasoning were followed in arriving at this conclusion. For 23 of the 30 traits he measured, Herskovits found information on other populations indi-

68

cating that the American Negro series showed low comparative variability. In 10 of these traits the American Negro series stood high on variability, in 6 it was at or near the bottom, and in 7 it was in the center of the list (*ibid.*, 20).

The other method of testing homogeneity consisted of a comparison of the variability of family lines with the variability within families. Extensive inbreeding within a population occasions a low variability of family lines because each of the families has approximately the same ancestry. Contrariwise, where there has been free mixture of all types within a people, the variability of the family lines is large. Also important in determining the extent to which a population is homogenous or heterogeneous is the variability *within* families. In an inbred population that has come from a homogeneous stock, the variability *within* families, as well as the variability of family lines, is low. In an inbred population descended from quite different types, the variability of the family lines is low, but *within* families it is relatively high. After measuring a large number of sets of brothers and sisters (fraternities), Herskovits computed the variability of family lines and the variability *within* families for the cephalic index (the ratio of the maximum breadth of the head to the maximum length), the only trait for which comparative material was available. A comparison of his data with the findings of studies of ten ethnic groups in the United States and other countries showed the results that had been hypothesized (1928, 27–28). To check the results obtained with the use of the cephalic index, Herskovits calculated the variabilities for the same fraternities for four traits in which there are known differences between Africans and Whites—interpupillary distance, nose width, height of ear, and length of middle finger. In every case, the variability of the family lines was smaller than that *within* the families (1928, 32).[2]

The inbreeding of the socially isolated American Negro population was likened to that of a geographically isolated group, and his

[2] Herskovits defended his studies in physical anthropology against criticisms of sampling in M. J. Herskovits, Vivian K. Cameron, and Harriet Smith, "The Physical Form of Mississippi Negroes," *American Journal of Physical Anthropology* 16 (1931): 193–201.

genealogical material led Herskovits to conclude that there was a progressive lessening of intermixture of American Negro people with the white and Indian populations. Only about two percent of the college generation in his sample knew of white parentage, but approximately ten percent knew of white grandparents and those who could trace their ancestry farther back gave even larger percentages.

Herskovits' interest in the intermixture of American Negroes and Whites did not end with the measurement of physical traits and the computation of variabilities of family lines and of those within families. One of the aspects of the acculturative process in the United States needing investigation was the extent of the advantages held by Negroes whose physical form was nearest that of the dominant white group. This question involved the effects of acculturation on the physical form as well as the attitudes of the American Negro. When each man in the Howard University series was asked whether his mother or his father was lighter in skin color, the following results were obtained:

Father lighter	*30.3 percent*
About the same color	*13.2 percent*
Mother lighter	*56.5 percent*

The results of the measurement of skin color in a large number of Harlem families—families from all parts of the United States as well as from the West Indies—confirmed the reports obtained from the men at Howard University. The percentages for these skin color observations were:

Husband lighter	*29.0 percent*
About the same color	*14.5 percent*
Wife lighter	*56.5 percent*

Herskovits' interpretation of these data was that Negro men, like men in general, seek as marriage partners women who will bring them prestige, and that cultural conditioning had conferred prestige on that which is non-Negroid. Social selection, then, was held to exert an influence on the development of biological type. If continued, this strong tendency toward marriage between dark men and light women, Herskovits said, would result in more Negroid features for the American Negro population in the future (1930b, 280).

Herskovits hypothesized that man's domestication had been a deciding factor in the formation of numerous varieties of human beings in today's world, and that through the mixture of a number of types a new type such as the American Negro might be formed. Since he found that in many traits the average for the American Negro was about halfway between the averages for the white population and the African, Herskovits argued that the American Negro people represent a blend rather than a group characterized by a series of dominant and recessive traits according to simple Mendelian inheritance. Furthermore, it was said, there would have to be an increase in variability if the Mendelian hypothesis were to be borne out in this instance (1928, 77–81). Later, Herskovits said that if Mendelian principles "are to be said to apply, multiple factors must be assumed for each character" (1930b, 280).

The American Negro: A Study in Racial Crossing ends on this note:

And what of our good word "race"? Are we any nearer to an understanding of what it means? Only, I think, in a negative sense. If race means anything in the way of a definite physical type, then the American Negro is a racial group. If it means anything in the sense that lowness of variation is associated with racial purity, then the American Negro is a pure racial group. But I do not claim the term "race" for the American Negro, and I certainly do not claim that there is anything but the most striking type of mixture represented in him. If anything, the theoretical significance of the work which has been presented in these discussions seems to be that it furnishes a dramatic illustration of how little we are able to define a word that has played such an important role in our political and social life, while it further illustrates how much we take for granted in the field of the genetic analysis of human populations. (1928, 81–82)

Finally, Herskovits' work in physical anthropology came at the beginning of his career; it was never the main thrust of his intellectual interest. His studies in this field, nevertheless, were well conceived, important, and are still valued.

VII ETHNOPSYCHOLOGY

Psychology. Herskovits' first publication applying psychological concepts to African and New World Negro cultures was "Freudian Mechanisms in Negro Psychology" (1934, 75–84). He held that in Negro cultures there existed a recognition of the nature of the mechanisms of repression and compensation, "and of the value of bringing a repressed thought into the open, though the explanation of the phenomenon is usually given in terms of the working of supernatural forces (*ibid.*, 77)." Moreover, instances of the practice of singing songs stating grievances against those in power are numerous in West African cultures and among New World Negroes. In Dahomey, the *avogan*, a marketplace dance, provides a socially institutionalized release for suppressed emotions. Crowds watch the dancing and enjoy the ridicule of those who have offended members of the quarter of Abomey giving the dance. Usually, names are not mentioned, not simply to prevent fighting, but because "the African relishes innuendo and circumlocution too well to be satisfied with bald, direct statement." Songs sung by one cowife to expose the misdeeds of another are common in Dahomey, as are those which make sport of Whites.

In the coastal region of Surinam, the *lobi singi* is a type of ridicule which is directed most frequently against a woman who has taken a man away from a rival. Or it may take place following a quarrel between two women working in a compound-yard. Such an event is well publicized, and spectators gather to listen to songs of the leader-and-chorus type and to watch the dancing. Although the words and melody are traditional, everyone present knows who is being criticized and understands perfectly the ritual of recrimination that is being staged (Herskovits and Herskovits, 1936, 23–25). Other examples of using songs for critical purposes include commentaries on rich men in Haiti (1934a, 75), and the songs on current social happenings and pompous people in Trinidad (Herskovits and Herskovits, 1947b, 276–79).

72

In traditional Dahomean thought, compensation through rationalization is seen in the explanation of national misfortunes on grounds other than the powerlessness of the gods and the ancestors. Thus, a smallpox epidemic or a locust plague "is a punishment meted out for the misdeeds of the living, for a breach against supernatural decrees. Defeat in a battle comes as punishment for violating the edict of an ancient ancestor that there be peace; the conquest of the French is accounted for by the fact that King Glele, the father of that Behanzin who was the reigning monarch when the French took Dahomey, had advised his son against war, and especially against war with the Whites who were the makers of implements of war— guns and gunpowder . . ." (1934a, 82–83).

Spirit possession interested Herskovits during his first trips to Surinam and to Dahomey, but his early field reports were limited to descriptive accounts of this phenomenon. In Brazil, he encountered the same popular theory of possession as elsewhere, and the same general type of behavior during the possession trance. In addition, however, he observed *éré* possession, an interesting type of semi-possession. He referred to this intermediate state as the "childishness which goes with every god" (1943c, 505). Other observers have also noted differences in depth of the state of dissociation.[1]

Herskovits said that the phenomenon of spirit possession cannot be equated with certain neurotic and psychotic manifestations of abnormality found in Western societies (1948b, 66–68). Although possession trance involves hysterical behavior, it cannot be regarded simply as hysteria. Herskovits pointed out that possession experiences are *culturally* patterned, often induced by learning and discipline, and that the acts of possessed persons are so stylized that the initiated can identify the god possessing a devotee by the behavior of the possessed person. Among investigators who have provided additional documentation on this point are Stainbrook (1952, 334), Ribeiro (1960, 2), and Bourguignon (1968, 35–36).

In his study of the *vodun* cult in Haiti, Herskovits noted that spirit

[1] See Messenger (1959), Anang Ibibio in Nigeria; Ribeiro (1960), Shango cult in Recife, Brazil; Bastide (1960), Brazil; Simpson (1962), Shango cult in Trinidad; and Henney (1968), Shakers in St. Vincent.

Melville J. Herskovits

possession gave release from psychic tension and offered a way to satisfy unfulfilled desires (1937b, 147). In Brazil, he had observed that this psychological catharsis took "the form of the resolution of a guilt feeling or other personality conflict, especially through the confession compelled of a devotee, while under possession by his deity. . . . The compulsion toward confession of conduct not socially sanctioned is projected onto the god and is thus achieved without distortion of the individual's ego-image or the destruction of those rationalizations which soften a sense of guilt at his misconduct" (1952d, 159). Later investigators have commented further on the compensatory nature of possession trance.[2]

Ribeiro says if an individual's temperament is not like that of a deity that possesses him, the problem is to determine "how far unconscious identification has effected change in him" (Ribeiro, 1949, 119–20). Bourguignon points out that analogies have been made between trance experiences and religious conversion on the one hand, and brainwashing on the other, "bringing about as they do an alteration of attitudes, memory functions, world view or self-concept" (Bourguignon, 1968, 57). As Bourguignon indicates, possession trance may also occur outside rituals. In situations of crisis and fear, the protective spirit appears to help the individual overcome pain and fear (Bourguignon, 1970, 90).

In 1948, Herskovits distinguished between socialization, "the process by means of which an individual is integrated into his society," and enculturation, "the means whereby an individual, during his entire lifetime, assimilates the traditions of his group and functions in terms of them" (1948b, 38, 491).[3] Socialization was con-

2 W. and F. Mischel list the following psychotherapeutic aspects of possession phenomena in the Shango cult in Trinidad: a degree of control over others that the possessed person does not possess in everyday life; the acting out of aggressive and sexual behavior; reversal of sex roles; temporary freedom of responsibility for actions (Mischel and Mischel, 1958, 254–56). For some people living under oppressive circumstances, possession provides catharsis. For persons living in other situations, it may reduce social tensions. Ribeiro found that the psychological consequences of spirit possession may be salutary or the opposite (Ribeiro, 1960, 7, 10, 13).
3 Whiting points out that the concept of "socialization" came to be used in the 1930s to denote the process by which culture is transmitted from generation to

ceived of as the achievement by one individual of a position in relation to the fellow-members of his group. He thought of enculturation as proceeding on two levels.

> *During early life, a person is conditioned to the basic patterns of the culture in accordance with which he is to live. He learns to handle the verbal symbols that make up his language, he masters accepted forms of etiquette, is inculcated with the ends of living recognized by his fellows, is adjusted to the established institutions of his culture. In all this he has but little to say; he is the instrument rather than the player. In later years, however, enculturation involves reconditioning rather than conditioning. The learning process is one wherein choice can operate, wherein what is presented can be accepted or rejected. (1948b, 491)*

Herskovits linked the mechanism of enculturation to the question of conservatism and change in culture by saying that the first level of the enculturative process gives stability to a culture, while enculturation on the conscious level "opens the gate to change, making for the examination of alternate possibilities, and permitting reconditioning modes of thought and conduct" (1948b, 491).

One aspect of Herskovits' concern with the enculturative experience was his interest in that part of socially sanctioned behavior that rests on a psychological plane below the level of consciousness (1952d, 153–56). Among the types of behavior on this level are linguistic patterns, motor habits of all kinds (walking, gesture used to accompany speech, work habits, such as those referred to in chapter 3 of the present work); aesthetic patterns, including those mentioned in chapter 4; and value systems, including those discussed in chapter 3.

---

generation, but that researchers have never been satisfied with this term, "in part because of its ambiguous connotations and in part because it suggests that the concept is limited to learning of social roles" (Whiting, 1968, 545). Whiting states that this implied exclusion of the transmission of beliefs and values led Kluckhohn (1939) to propose "culturalization" and Herskovits (1948b) to suggest "enculturation" to cover this conceptual inadequacy. Since the term "child rearing" also fails to suggest cultural transmission, the conceptual problem in this area has not been resolved.

Herskovits had a special interest in the implications and the opportunities that the Afroamerican field holds for research in the area of culture and personality. In addition to his examination of the mechanisms of repression, compensation, and catharsis, and of the nature of the enculturative process, he thought that study of the conventions of child care would help to explain personality differences between, for example, the Bush Negroes of Surinam and the peasants of Haiti. He was also interested in the possibilities of using projective techniques to determine the modal personality structure of a people (1952d, 156–58).

Examining the Oedipus theme in the course of their study of oral tradition in Dahomey, the Herskovitses developed the thesis that "the emphasis laid in many discussions of myth on the Oedipus theme of the hostility of the son toward his father has caused certain major psychocultural factors that enter into the broader competitive configurations of human social life, to be overlooked" (Herskovits and Herskovits, 1958b, 1). Their analysis took into account the more inclusive mechanisms of generation and sibling rivalry. Specifically, in analyzing the forces underlying the elements of myth included in the Oedipus category, they found it necessary to consider the father's fear of being displaced by his son, as well as the son's jealousy of the father. In their hypothesis, "the father's jealousy of the son can be conceptualized as the aspect of the sibling rivalry complex which, through projection, reactivates the infantile competition for the mother in terms of competition for the affection of the wife, who is the mother of his son" (*ibid.*, 14). Numerous instances were given of strife between brothers in Dahomean narrative forms, and the culture provides patterned sanctions for the resolution of parental anxieties in the face of certain types of challenge from their children. Those born with gross abnormalities, a child born with teeth, or one whose upper teeth appear before the lower, or a child who is born after twins, are believed to be a threat to the parents, or even to the whole group. Examples of resentment against the father are found in Dahomean myths, but such hostility is not handled by parricide. Thus, the evidence from cross-cultural data presented by the Herskovitses,

76

and their analysis of these data, extended rather than ruled out the Oedipus theorem (*ibid.*, 14).

Herskovits hypothesized that cultural differences might be of such magnitude as to influence perceptual tendencies. Over a period of time, Herskovits debated this question with Donald Campbell, a psychologist at Northwestern University, with the latter taking the position that "the biological homogeneity of culture-learning man would preclude such influence" (Segall, Campbell, and Herskovits, 1966, vi). In 1956, it was decided to do field work on this issue with appropriate psychological instruments and techniques. Many, but not all, of the data were collected in Africa. This study revealed

> *significant differences across cultures in susceptibility to several geometric, or optical, illusions. It should be stressed that these differences are not "racial" differences. They are differences produced by the same kinds of factors that are responsible for individual differences in illusion susceptibility, namely, differences in experience. The findings we have reported, and the findings of others we have reviewed, point to the conclusion that to a substantial extent we learn to perceive; that in spite of the phenomenally absolute character of our perceptions, they are determined by perceptual inference habits; and that various inference habits are differentially likely in different societies. For all mankind, the basic process of perception is the same, only the contents differ and these differ only because they reflect different perceptual inference habits. (Segall, Campbell, and Herskovits, 213–14)*

Rhoda Métraux finds that the Segall, Campbell, and Herskovits conclusions confirm and extend W. H. R. Rivers' studies of the early 1900s. (Rivers found systematic differences between the Murray Islanders and the Toda on the one hand, and his samples of English adults and children on the other, in susceptibility to two types of illusion.) She adds that the more recent research is important in its own right, in part because it brings together the collaboration of representatives of two disciplines on a problem of common interest (Métraux, 1969, 370–71).

Education. Herskovits' interest in psychology led to a consideration of education and the learning process in relation to cultural transmission and cultural change. He was concerned with the educative process by means of which African custom was transmitted from one generation to the next in Africa, but he gave attention also to the role of this process in maintaining cultural stability and promoting cultural change in New World Negro social behavior.

In Herskovits' accounts of child-training in Dahomey, the closeness of contact between mother and child is noteworthy. During the child's first year, it is seldom away from its mother. After three or four months, the ordinary mother returns to work in the fields or walks along the road obtaining goods to sell in the market, with the child "always astride her back, or near by" (1943a, 740). Discipline and affection are mixed in training the child to eat whatever is presented to it and to control its excretory functions. The child is about a year old when it learns to walk. Afterward, it receives training in the routine of daily life.

Training in the occupations of one's elders begins early in Dahomey. A girl of five accompanies her mother to market; at ten or eleven she can cook all of the staple foods used in a household. Boys from four to nine assist in ironworking, and both boys and girls help with the planting by the time they are nine or ten. Until the age of seven, however, a child spends most of the day in play, and meets with other children in the evenings for storytelling. Since many of the tales include morals, the elders believe that storytelling is an efficacious way of indoctrinating children (1938b, 1: 275–76; 1943a, 742). At the age of eight, a boy becomes a "partridge-chaser-person" and goes to the fields with his father to try to prevent the birds from harming the seeds or the crops. At the same age a girl becomes a "things-peddle-person" who goes about the village or market place trying to sell soap, chewing sticks, salt or sugar. At ten or eleven, boys are called "wood-throw-lizard" to designate the middle period of childhood, when their motor control enables them to kill a lizard. At this time, girls are called "woman-small," and sex education begins for both boys and girls. Boys no longer sleep in their mothers' houses; they construct their own with those of their age in the compound.

Girls of this age continue to sleep in the houses of their mothers or, frequently, in those of their paternal grandmothers. Sex education is given to girls from nine to twelve in groups of a dozen or less by a married woman between twenty-five and thirty years of age. Boys dramatize the stories told in their house by simulating the experiences of sex. Conversations with an elder brother or paternal male cousin increase a boy's sex knowledge, and discussions of sex occur frequently in the boys' house. Groups of boys and girls meet clandestinely at night to play typical Dahomean children's games. Several months of these preliminary events may take place before intercourse occurs. For the girls, the ensuing period of sex experimentation ceases at the attainment of puberty and the ceremonies that mark this occasion (1938b, vol. 1, ch. 14).

In addition to the training in occupational techniques that a child receives in the prepuberty period, two other kinds of conditioning are important in his development. First, observation and experience of the manner of life of his elders provide training in the proper behavior towards others and some knowledge of religious and ceremonial custom. Although the rites related to his own birth occur too early to affect his behavior or personality structure, later he observes these ceremonies as they are performed for younger siblings in his compound. Such rites, as well as his observation of the major ceremonies of his village, impress upon the child the need for supernatural sanctions in most of life's situations. The other strand in the educational experiences of the child during this stage of life is the atmosphere of a polygynous compound. "Factors of sexual rivalry, of jockeying for position, of attaining preference for a child, make for intrigue that goes on against a background of shifting alliances between co-wives which reveals the inner drama of such groupings" (1943a, 743).

Acknowledging that the degree of variation in individual reactions to the learning process is not easy to determine, Herskovits characterizes the Dahomean, on the whole, as one who

> accepts the stratified forms of social structure that mark the culture, manifesting at the same time ambition to attain prestige in recognized ways, and having a drive to take advantage of

79

Melville J. Herskovits

such avenues of social mobility as may present themselves. At the same time, the individual is trained to cooperate with his fellows and, as a result of the overt characterization of the ways of life, to have an objectively manifested affection for and pride in his people and the institutions by which they live. He shows his reserve in his dealings with others, but in certain situations, particularly when dealing with those who stand in the relation of institutionalized friendship to him or with members of his own cult group or association, he manifests a warmth of regard and a willingness to aid in difficulties that compensate for these other characteristics. Certainly, whatever the stability of such a psychological type, the effectiveness of the training given in carrying on the institutional aspects of Dahomean life from generation to generation have been demonstrated by perpetuating this culture for many generations and by performing well the task of adequately adjusting those who live in accordance with its sanctions. (1943a, 744)

In a discussion of "Education and Cultural Dynamics," Herskovits coupled an analysis of the socialization process in Dahomey with the role that education has had in the New World in contributing to the retention or disappearance of African habit patterns and institutionalized forms of behavior. In doing this, he again challenged a common assumption that African modes of behavior have disappeared in the Diaspora. Although a certain dilution in African behavior was bound to occur in the new environment, Herskovits said "it is difficult to see how it would have been possible for a slave to bring up his children without inculcating in them something of the values of life and the modes of behavior that he had in Africa been taught to regard as right and proper" (1943a, 745). This teaching would have included the unconscious imitation by the children of habits that lay beneath the level of consciousness—habits of speech behavior and motor behavior of various kinds. We point out in the chapter on the New World Negro that the degree of carry-over of African traits varies in the areas of technology, economic life, political organization, social organization, religion, magic, and art. An analysis of the retention of African cultural elements must be accompanied by a study of "how the European patterns of behavior manifested by Negroes today, and their non-African sanctions, were established" (1943a, 745–47). As mentioned earlier, it was Herskovits' belief that the behavior and customs of New World Negroes could be understood only in terms of three variables: the background of West African traditions, the conditions of life during slavery, and the socioeconomic status of Afro-Americans since freedom (1941a, 8, 136, 180–81).

VIII THEORY AND METHOD

Herskovits' concerns with ethnological theory and method were accompanied by an interest in the history of anthropology. His articles on developments in anthropology in the United States and in European countries (1927b, 12–13; 1944a, 64–65; 1945a, 54–55; 1945b, 639–41; 1946a, 55–57; 1946b, 301–4; 1947, 120–26; and 1959e, 389–98) dealt with the publication of important books and monographs, the starting of new journals, the launching of new programs of studies, the contributions of anthropologists to the problems related to World War II and the postwar period, the adoption of landmark resolutions by the American Anthropological Association, the effects of the war on anthropology and anthropologists in France, Belgium, and Holland, the history of "schools" of thought in ethnology from the time of the classical evolutionists to 1959, and the problems of graduate training in anthropology.[1]

Perhaps the main contribution that Herskovits made to the history of the science was his biography and assessment of Boas' work (1953).[2] Boas' influence on Herskovits' thinking and career is apparent. Herskovits' early interest in Africa was stimulated by Boas' inquiry into the role of kinship terminology in maintaining social sanctions among the Vandau, and his extensive work in physical

[1] In view of the numerous discussions of the problems of anthropological research and ethics in recent years, Herskovits' comments on one aspect of training students for foreign field trips are of special interest. "The officials of the foreign office of the country he is visiting, the local administrative and police officials of the community where he works, must be told, fully and honestly, of his plans, his ends, his methods" (1949b, 522). Coincidentally, Herskovits succeeded in maintaining a balance between friendship with nationalist leaders in Africa and proper relations with the colonial governments, relations that were essential if his students were to have access to the field.
[2] For the latest study of Boas, see Alexander Lesser's *Franz Boas*, a forthcoming volume in the Leaders of Modern Anthropology Series, Columbia University Press.

anthropology in the early part of his career followed the pattern of Boas' studies of physical type. Herskovits' lifelong commitment to the historical rather than the ahistorical approach in cultural anthropology is traceable to Boas' theoretical position. Culture change, one of Herskovits' major theoretical and empirical concerns, was a problem of great interest to Boas. Herskovits' interest in psychological anthropology may be attributed, in part at least, to Boas' emphasis on the reciprocal influence of culture and human behavior. In addition, it seems probable that Herskovits' interest in the influence of culture on perception and his interest in the question of the retention of Africanisms in motor habits among the people of the Caribbean was related to Boas' interests in such matters. Similar comments seem to apply to the interests of teacher and student in aesthetics and language.[3] Although Boas did not employ the term "cultural relativism," this principle was a part of his thinking.[4] Herskovits' eclecticism was similar to Boas', as were his field methods (*ibid.*, 22–23, 75–80). Finally, the two men were close together on the question of the application of scientific findings to practical affairs (*ibid.*, 106).

Acculturation. Some of Herskovits' theoretical interests—for example, enculturation—have been referred to in earlier chapters. He was

[3] In the controversy concerning myth as validation of belief or as the expression of symbolisms, Boas took the first position, Herskovits wrote: "So strong was his set against any explanation of symbolism except on the level of explicit cultural interpretation that he cut himself off from certain insights a cross-cultural application of such a concept as that of the unconscious might yield. Work that has been done since his death strengthens his position as to the lack of validity of symbols drawn in terms of universal equivalents. But it has also become apparent that if considered within the rubric of the culture, the analysis of unconscious symbols can be carried on with very real profit. Nor can the question of the broader validity of certain symbols, that can conceivably arise from common reactions of man to certain constants in human experience, be dismissed as summarily as Boas was wont to dismiss it" (1953, 91).
[4] Herskovits quoted this statement by Boas: ". . . it is certainly conceivable that there may be other civilizations, based perhaps on different traditions and on a different equilibrium of emotion and reason which are of no less value than ours, although it may be impossible for us to appreciate their influence. The general theory of valuation of human activities, as developed by anthropological research, teaches us a higher tolerance than the one we now profess" (*ibid*, 101).

eclectic in theory, with his strongest interests centering in culture change, ethnohistory, and cultural relativism.

In 1945, Herskovits drew together the attempts anthropologists had made to explain the processes of cultural change (1945d, 143–70). He compared the historical approach of Boas, Nordenskiöld, Kroeber, Spier, and others, with the German and English distributional schools. He pointed out that a reaction to the latter schools came in the nonhistorical approach of Malinowski, Firth, Fortune, and others. Herskovits considered the essentially static approach of the functionalists as inadequate when analysis moved from relatively isolated, stable cultures to research in areas where societies were in contact with European communities or had been influenced considerably by European custom (*ibid.*, 149–50). To understand what had occurred in Africa, Australia, or in some parts of Melanesia influenced by Europe, he argued that it was necessary to establish a historical base line from which change had started. Herskovits' statement of the problems involved in studying culture change was succinct.

> *Changes in a culture are effected by innovations introduced from within and from without. Changes initiated from within take the form of inventions or discoveries; those from without are due to borrowing. In either case, the crucial problem is whether or not the element newly presented will be accepted or rejected. If rejected, it of course disappears, but if accepted, it is then important to determine, so far as possible, the mechanisms by which it was incorporated into the existing body of custom that accepted it, particularly whether it was taken over in its entirety or partially accepted, and how it was changed when being integrated into the accepting culture. (1945d, 150–51)*

Much insight can be gained, Herskovits said, through the study of variations in custom among historically related peoples, or within subgroups of a large population, or through the changes that can be shown to have occurred over a certain time period (*ibid.*, 162–63).

Herskovits felt that preoccupation with the outer forms of culture

83

had resulted in an inadequate search for its psychological significance. Insisting that the ultimate reality of culture is psychological, he saw in this reality the mechanisms of both cultural stability and cultural change—reality in the ease that human beings find in living under a known routine, and reality because the differing aptitudes and interests of individual members operating within their cultural matrix produce continuous revisions in existing custom (1945d, 163).

Herskovits' first publication on acculturation, "Acculturation and the American Negro" (1927a) dealt with the acceptance by Negro Americans of certain values held by the numerically dominant population. Among such values he listed one hundred percent Americanism, seen in the attitude of the American-born Negro to West Indian Negroes; the hostility toward spirituals on the part of well-to-do Negroes prior to the late 1920s; the condescending attitude of Negro Americans toward African wood carving; and the color preferences revealed by American Negroes in the selection of marriage partners (*ibid.*, 217-19). Von Hornbostel's testimony concerning the influence of European culture on the form of the spiritual was cited as further evidence of the acculturation of the American Negro (*ibid.*, 221-24).

The well-known and influential "Memorandum for the Study of Acculturation" was published by Robert Redfield, Ralph Linton, and Herskovits in 1935-36 in *Man, American Journal of Sociology, American Anthropologist, Africa,* and *Oceania.*[5]

[5] In the history of American anthropology, a discussion of the appropriateness of publishing papers on acculturation in the *American Anthropologist* is of considerable interest. At the annual meeting of the American Anthropological Association in 1936, Leslie Spier, editor of the *American Anthropologist,* said: "The question has also arisen how far we should go in printing material on the culture of natives who participate in civilized life. I have reference here to the so-called acculturation studies. It is maintained on the one hand that studies of such hybrid cultures are best left to sociological or other journals concerned with aspects of modern life; on the other, that they belong in the *American Anthropologist.* Since your wishes should be followed, I would like an expression of your opinion of what we should include.

"It was moved and seconded: It is the sense of the American Anthropological Association that papers in the field of acculturation lie within the interests of anthropology, and that, at the Editor's discretion, they be not discriminated against in the *American Anthropologist.* It was voted that the motion be tabled

Herskovits believed that most students of nonliterate peoples are oblivious to historical records bearing on the cultures they study. He argued that studies of acculturation require recourse to actual recorded history, not historical reconstructions. For example, in Haiti investigators had been able to identify the African tribes that contributed to the Negro ancestry of the present population, and thus to the African elements in the culture of that country. Likewise, historical analysis had made it possible to indicate the cultural configuration the French presented to the slaves (1937d, 262). Among the many specific problems in cultural change that Herskovits said could best be studied through analyses of acculturation were the relative conservatism of men and women, the mechanisms that enable an individual to further or to retard cultural change, and the educative forces which condition an individual to traditional patterns of behavior (*ibid.*, 262).

In 1938, Herskovits published *Acculturation: The Study of Culture Contact*, an exhaustive analysis of the subject. In this work, he attempted first to clarify the meaning of the term.

> *For some the word seems to imply the meaning inherent in its earliest uses—the result of somewhat close contact between peoples resulting in a give-and-take of their cultures; for others it appears to hold the significance implicit in Powell's usage of 1900 —the process whereby a specific trait is ingested by a recipient culture; while still others apparently accept it as the means whereby an individual "becomes acculturated" to the patterns of his own society, a usage that makes the term "acculturation" a synonym for "education"* (1938a, 6).

Herskovits left no doubt about his endorsement of the meaning given first in this series. He then quoted the definition given in the "Outline on Acculturation" published in 1935–1936 by the Sub-Com-

---

without prejudice." ("Proceedings of the American Anthropological Association," *American Anthropologist* 39 [1937]: 322.) Regardless of that motion, the issues of the *American Anthropologist* soon included numerous studies on acculturation.

mittee of the Social Science Research Council of which he was a member. According to that definition: "Acculturation comprehends those phenomena which result when groups of individuals having different cultures come into continuous first-hand contact, with subsequent changes in the original practices of either or both groups." To this definition a note was appended as an integral part of the statement:

> . . . acculturation is to be distinguished from cultural-change, of which it is but one aspect, and assimilation,[6] which is at times a phase of acculturation. It is also to be differentiated from diffusion, which, while occurring in all instances of acculturation, is not only a phenomenon which frequently takes place without the occurrence of the types of contact between peoples specified in the definition given above, but also constitutes only one aspect of the process of acculturation.

Concerning the use of the word "traits" in the Outline on Acculturation, Redfield had asked whether, in analyzing a culture that has been subjected to an acculturative process, one should be content with a "sorting-process into one of two pigeon-holes" (Redfield, 1934, 58, 61; quoted in Herskovits, 1938a, 28). On this point Herskovits commented:

> In a given culture, the assignment of one element or another to a specific source merely clears the ground so that we can understand the kinds of things that were taken over or rejected, the ways in which they were integrated into the culture, and, from this and the study of many acculturative situations, of the possibility of working out general principles of cultural change. (1938a, 28–29)

In 1937, Herskovits raised an objection to one of the points in the definition given in the joint memorandum; namely, the phrase "groups of individuals." Studies such as his investigation of Haitian

---

[6] For recent discussions of the concept of assimilation, see Gordon (1964, 70–71), and Simpson (1968, 438).

culture, "concerned with a people whose ascertainable past history shows the effect of first-hand, continued contact between two cultures" had come, he said, to be regarded as acculturation studies (1937b, 323). Later (1941b, 7), he suggested that the memorandum definition he rephrased "so as to emphasize the continuous nature of the cultural impulses from the donor to the receiving groups, whether these be at first hand or through literary channels." Such rephrasing would also permit the definition to cover situations of acculturation where

> first-hand contact is continuous, but whose carriers are of a special class, such as government administrators or missionaries or traders, where sex ratios of the incoming groups are abnormal, or where other conditions cause the native to experience European tradition in less than its rounded form. It is recognized that in such situations complete "coverage" cannot be obtained; that, however, the printed or written word can transmit far more of the donor culture than the group of a particular sex or a particular occupation could ever of itself give has not been similarly recognized. (1941b, 7) [7]

Herskovits realized that neither duration nor intensity of contact can provide adequate criteria for distinguishing acculturation from other types of cultural change. Where the concern is with the processes of cultural change, it seemed to him that it is of little importance whether a particular case of cultural transmission is called acculturation or diffusion. He thought it useful to differentiate between diffusion as the study of achieved cultural transmission, and acculturation as the study of cultural transmission in process (1948b, 525). Instead of Malinowski's concept of the "zero-point" in culture, the point from which change in an assumed static way of life began, Herskovits favored the use of a "base-line," some period in the history of a given culture antecedent to the particular contact being investigated and

[7] Linton distinguished between "directed culture change" and a situation "in which members of a society are able to choose cultural elements freely" (Linton, 1940; Spicer, 1968, 22).

therefore a point from which change could be triangulated (*ibid.*, 528).

By the middle 1960s, the term "modernization" was being used in some ethnological studies to characterize phenomena that had formerly come under the rubric "acculturation." Also, some research-grant–dispensing agencies, as well as some political leaders in developing countries, began to favor this term. It is, however, harder to define precisely and objectively than is acculturation. Modernization is a goal in some situations where acculturation is occurring, but the concept is more limited and value-laden than acculturation.

The meaning of acculturation and related concepts may be summarized as follows:

DIFFUSION: (1) cultural change brought about in the absence of direct contact; (2) achieved cultural transmission.

ACCULTURATION: (1) cultural change occasioned by prolonged contacts, face to face or through communications media, "between representatives of different societies or between ethnic enclaves and their encompassing societies"; [8] (2) cultural transmission in process.

ETHNOHISTORY: "the use of historical documents to provide time-depth to ethnographic observations" (1952a, 53).

MODERNIZATION: the processes and changes regarded as essential to transform a developing, nonindustrial people into a society that can take its place among the family of nations in the contemporary world.

Two central concepts in Herskovits' thinking about acculturation were cultural focus and reinterpretation. By cultural focus he meant "that phenomenon which gives a culture its particular emphasis; which permits the outsider to sense its special distinguishing flavor . . ." (1945c, 21). He viewed focus as "the tendency of every culture to exhibit greater variation in the institutions of some of its aspects

[8] S.S.R.C. (1954, 974). The Summer Seminar on Acculturation, 1953, distinguished such contacts from those "resulting from the interactions of factions, classes, occupational groups, or other special categories within a single society. . . . Socialization, urbanization, industrialization, and secularization are not acculturation processes unless they are cross-culturally introduced rather than intraculturally developed phenomena."

than in others" (1948b, 542). Typifying this tendency is the emphasis on supernatural validating agencies in the cultures of West Africa and of New World Negroes. Herskovits cited the importance in Africa of supernatural sanctions for those involved in trade, in agricultural pursuits, in the political order and in aesthetic activities —wood carving, singing, and storytelling (1945d, 165–66). Likewise, a strong interest in religion is manifest in people of African descent in the New World, even in modern cities in Brazil, the West Indies, and the United States.[9]

Herskovits defined reinterpretation as "the process by which old meanings are ascribed to new elements or by which new values change the cultural significance of old forms" (1948b, 553). Africans in the New World and in Africa have done, he said, what peoples under contact always do.

> If they are under restraint, they retain as much of an earlier tradition as the new situation in which they find themselves permits. Where they can make their choices freely, they accept innovations to the degree that these new elements are in consonance with their pre-existing patterns. For the most part, whatever freedom of choice they may have, they respond by retaining meaning and value, casting these in new forms, through a process which I have designated as reinterpretation. This is what Africans and their descendants did; and this . . . is what we can see Africans doing in Africa itself. (1959c, 234)

From the point of view of the individual in a situation of cultural contact, Herskovits saw four kinds of response to new cultural stimuli: "syncretism; where identification is not as clear, reinterpretation results; and where there is a minimum of concurrence, the additive

[9] An interesting instance of cultural focus is speech behavior in St. Vincent, West Indies (Abrahams and Bauman, 1971, 762). This behavior "is unquestionably a principal focus of attention for the Vincentians themselves, and the amount of talk one hears about talk on the island is truly striking. Talking, in fact, bears all the earmarks among the Vincentian peasants of a cultural focus, in the classic sense of the word (Herskovits, *Cultural Anthropology*, 1955a, 485)"

factor comes into play, unless an innovation is rejected out of hand"
(*ibid.*, 235).

Herskovits regarded syncretism as a process where some of the old
and new cultural elements "are merged into a functioning unified
entity of clear bi-cultural derivation" (1952c, 57). In the New
World, this form is found most strikingly in the reconciliations
that have been effected by people of African descent in the field of
religion. An outstanding example of such syncretisms is the identification, in Catholic countries of the New World, of African deities
with the saints of the Church (1948b, 553; and see selection 9); or
where retention of the tribal deities was not possible, certain ritual
forms, such as possession, baptism, and curing in connection with
worship were continued (1945d, 167).

In 1959, Herskovits said that cases of syncretism were difficult to
find in Africa. Examples of reinterpretation, however, were numerous.

In the political sphere an assembly of clan elders develops
into a local government body, retaining antecedent patterns of
discussion and decision making, but with the complex as a whole
set within a new framework of authority. On the economic level,
the private ownership of trees, which is tradition, may serve as
a bridge towards the reinterpretation of earlier conventions of land
tenure, rationalizing individual ownership of the land itself. An
instance . . . where the complex of destoolment [the removal of
a ruler from office] in Ghana was applied to the dismissal of a
trades union official, offers a further example of the functioning
of the reinterpretative mechanism. . . . We can see the same
phenomenon at work where the Ibo family and lineage contribute
toward the cost of higher education for members who show
promise as scholars, reinterpreting a pre-existing sanction for the
extension of economic aid to those who take titles (1959c, 235–36).

In the field of religion, studies of the Separatist churches in South
Africa, the new cults in Central Africa, the independent religious
groups in East and West Africa, and the Islamic separatism of the
Moslem Brotherhoods have demonstrated "the ways worked out by

the peoples of Africa to maintain underlying sanctions of belief and behavior under cultural change" (*ibid.*, 236). Researches into these developments have shown important economic and political implications as well as the religious and moral ones.

Using the base-line discussed earlier, Herskovits organized the materials of New World Negro cultures in terms of the historical framework. New World Africanisms were shown, country by country, on a scale of intensity from most African to least African (most European). The countries ranged from Guyana (bush) through Haiti (peasant and urban), Brazil (Bahia, Porto Alegre, urban north, rural north), Jamaica (Maroons, Morant Bay, other), Trinidad (Toco, Port-of-Spain), Cuba, Honduras (Black Carib), Virgin Islands, Gulla Islands, United States (rural South), United States (North), (1945c, 14; 1948b, 615; 1955a, 527). In the later versions of this scale, the degree of retention was given by aspect of culture rather than by whole cultures (1955a, 526–527). Retentions were found to be greatest in religion, magic, folklore, and music; least in technology, economic life, and art. Language, social structures based on kinship, and nonkinship institutions fell in the middle of the scale.

Herskovits thought that the hypotheses of cultural focus and of reinterpretation help to explain why a given people take over one new idea or thing presented to them and reject another (1948b, 560). The unique historical forces that are present in a given situation occasion different results in different instances as far as the various aspects of culture are concerned (1945c, 13). In the New World, pressures from outside the Negro groups militating against the retention of economic patterns were stronger than the pressures against the retention of folktales or secular musical forms, with the result that the latter two are far more African than the former. At the same time, Herskovits held, "inner compulsions derived from the focal concerns of Africans with the supernatural tended to resist varying pressures, in varying countries, employing the different kinds of adjustments, . . . with the result that Africanisms figure prominently in New World religious behavior everywhere" (*ibid.*, 13–14).

We referred earlier to Herskovits' hypothesis that elements of a culture that are carried below the level of consciousness have persisted among New World Negroes to a greater degree than in the case of those cultural elements which require thought or call for decision (1945c, 22). Such "cultural imponderables" include linguistic patterns and musical style, as well as sanctions underlying certain types of motor behavior, systems of values, and codes of etiquette, even though these elements lie outside the area of cultural focus.

Among the concepts that have been used in recent years in the study of the acculturative situation are boundary-maintaining mechanisms and role networks (S.S.R.C. Summer Seminar on Acculturation, 1953 [1954, 973–1002]). In 1968, Spicer pointed out that six foci of interest had developed among those interested in acculturation: "(a) nativistic movements, (b) cultural fusion, (c) personality and acculturation, (d) biculturism, (e) social scale and cultural change, and (f) techniques in directed change" (Spicer, 1968, 21–26). Crowley uses the term "creolization" to describe "more generally the processes of adaptation Herskovits synthesized as retention, reinterpretation and syncretism" (Crowley, quoted in Whitten and Szwed, 1970, 38). He says that the concept may be applied in any area of the world "where a culture neither aboriginal nor alien but a mixture of the two, with retentions on both sides and ample borrowing from other outside sources is in the process of becoming dominant—which is to say, most of the world." According to Crowley, "the term creole is no longer necessarily related to race." Although acculturation has become a standard word in the language of social science (A. Linton and Wagley, 1971, 52). There is disagreement among social scientists as to whether acculturation should be thought of as a distinctive type of culture change.

Ethnohistory. The ethnohistorical approach overlaps with acculturation studies (Hammond, 1971, 383). In 1952, Herskovits spoke of "the ethnohistoric study of acculturation" (1952d, 152–53). Ethnohistorians utilize oral traditions and written records to construct an account of a people's past, including a record of their contacts and conflicts with other groups. Herskovits regarded the use of historical documentation to provide time-depth to ethnographic observations as "a major methodological shift in the study of cultural dynamics" (1952c, 53). In addition to checking the facts concerning the pre-contact cultures, ethnohistory affords valuable details concerning the acceptance of new or retention of old ways, and gives some indication of the roles played by individuals and subgroupings during the process of culture change. (See also selection 6).

In an important paper published in 1936, Herskovits presented evidence gathered in the field, or which had appeared in recent historical publications, concerning the significance of West Africa for research on the Negro. Substantiation of the provenience of Negro populations residing in Surinam, Jamaica, Haiti, Brazil, and Cuba came in part from evidence that many of their place names, religious rites, names of deities, and social customs were derived from tribes living between Cape Three Points and the mouth of the Niger River. Another type of evidence concerning the derivation of slaves comes from the manifests of ships arriving at American ports from regions of West Africa and from Angola. Herskovits called attention also to the failure to find in such New World Negro cultures as those of the Guianas, Haiti, or Jamaica any significant trace of Senegalese or Congo traditions (1936b, 15–30; see also selection 5). The substantiation of the hypothesis that the area of the slave trade was, for the most part, West Africa rather than the whole continent, and of this region the coastal section rather than the deeper interior, is of great importance in the study of cultural dynamics among New World Negroes.

In a discussion of "Anthropology and Africa—A Wider Perspective," Herskovits said that anthropological research in Africa had been characterized by an intensive microethnographic approach which had emphasized institutions and their functions within a given society (1959c, 225). He urged Africanists to broaden their efforts by using distribution studies for the understanding of the historical relationships that have contributed to the making of given contemporary cultural situations and also to give more attention to the study of cultural dynamics. Mention was made of his classification of African culture areas and its uses, and his conclusion that "underlying local patterns made for regional differences in reaction to situations of contact . . ." (*ibid.*, 226–27). The work of Lindblom into the distributions of material cultural elements, as well as classifications of languages by Westermann, Werner, Greenberg, and others, was cited to show the value of comparative anthropological studies in Africa. Other examples of such work at that time had included the analyses of art provinces by Olbrechts, Wingert, Fagg, and others, of musical areas by Merriam, and of political systems by Fortes and Evans-Pritchard.

Even these broader investigations had, however, remained descriptive. What was needed, Herskovits argued, was some conceptual scheme for sorting out the data—geographical, stylistic, functional, or other (1959c, 228). In advocating the ethnohistorical approach, four kinds of resources were listed: those of history, archaeology, oral tradition, and ethnology (*ibid.*, 230).

Herskovits warned that distribution studies must be pursued within limited areas, and he said that reconstruction on the basis of ethnographic materials cannot show actual time of contact or the direction in which a given complex may have spread. He reminded ethnohistorians that another consideration to keep in mind is that "the spread of culture is not necessarily a function of the migration of peoples" (1959c, 232–33); that is, cultural borrowing may take place without ethnic displacement.

In contrasting the historical and the ahistorical approaches to Afroamerican studies, Herskovits asserted that in the former, the concept of culture is crucial, while in the latter, society is the organizing concept (1960a, 564). As an example of the ahistorical approach, he cited a study of the Negro family in Guyana, quoting passages from the Introduction:

> As social anthropologists, we are interested in the study of social structures as they exist over a limited time span, usually broad enough to enable us to discern and record regular customary modes of social action (R. T. Smith, 1956, 8). . . . The whole picture of the establishment of the free Negro villages is an exceedingly complex one and its detailed documentation in the wider

94

context of the social, economic, and political movements of the time remains a task for the historian. (*ibid.*, 13)

After tracing the history of the founding and development of the three villages included in this study, Smith says that, "We have no reason to believe that the 'culture' of the Negro villages has changed substantially over the last hundred years or so despite the continued 'culture contact' situation, and it will be part of our thesis that the peculiar 'culture' of the Negro villages is correlated with their structural position in the Guianese social system" (*ibid.*, 22). Herskovits commented that the synchronic analysis of structure can tell us what "a given system of relationships is at a given moment," but that it cannot answer "the question why they take their observed form. The ahistorical character of the structural approach makes it inevitable that at least one element in the 'why' equations, the time factor, is relegated to a minor place, if it is considered at all. In Afroamerican research, this means that components from Europe, Africa, and aboriginal America are neglected . . ." (1960a, 565–66).

Although many anthropologists recognized the importance of a knowledge of materials from the African areas from which New World Negroes were derived for studies in the Afroamerican field, Herskovits was the first to point out that gains could be had from applying the results of Afroamericanist research to Africanist studies (1948a, 1–10). His discussion included the usefulness of the theoretical postulates of cultural tenacity, cultural focus, and reinterpretation, as well as two methodological considerations. His first methodological point was that where New World Negroes have retained African cultural traits in relatively pure form, these are less complex than in Africa. Since the Africanist who is familiar with Afroamerican materials comes to the more complicated aboriginal parallels with an appreciation of their essentials, his studies can be phrased "in terms of a recognition of basic unities over a given area, and a perspective toward variants that can counteract descriptions of seemingly fragmented belief, or of amorphous practices, autonomous and unrelated to any common world view" (*ibid.*, 5). Secondly, the results of Afroamerican research were said to reveal structural unities in African culture that go beyond tribal groups and contiguous geographical localities to a view of West African and Congo cultures in general.

> In the experience of slavery, with rare exceptions, local variants could not be sustained. Differences that marked off one people from another tended to be "smoothed." The least common denominators of their cultures, however, were by this very fact forced to the surface, and where pressures were not rigid, those African elements which were incompatible with the values of the dominant group were suppressed (1948a, 6–7).

Among the reinterpretations of African custom found in Afroamerican cultures, Herskovits cited *wari* or *adji* as a New World finding that led to a reexamination of this game for ramifications that had not been studied before in Africa. Research in Bahia, Brazil, called attention to aspects of the role of the drummer in Africa that merited study by Africanists. The postpossession phenomenon called *eré* in Bahia and in Trinidad had been overlooked in Africanist studies (1948a, 9). Among other instances where Afroamerican materials have aided in Africanist research are the place of the noninitiate members of cult-groups; the symbolic significance of the three-year and seven-year ritual cycle following the death of an important officeholder, before his successor can take over in his own right; the pattern of improvisation, especially in arranging songs of praise and criticism as well as an incentive for creative effort; the tendency for the suppression of African religion to stimulate an increase in the use of magic; and the study of intertribal acculturation as an African tradition of adaptation (*ibid.*, 9–10).

Cultural Relativism. Herskovits' advocacy of cultural relativism precipitated many heated debates in the 1950s. The controversy over this concept attracted participants from many fields, including anthropology, sociology, philosophy, religion, social psychology, art, and

96

literature. In Herskovits' view, evaluations of conduct are relative to the cultural background out of which they arise. Judgments are based on experience, and experience is interpreted by each individual in terms of his own enculturation. No absolute moral standards exist for all peoples everywhere and at all times. Moral standards effectively channel conduct only insofar as they coincide with the orientations of a given people at a given period of their history (1948b, chap. 5). Secondly, and this is an extension of the first point, it is difficult to find criteria for evaluating ends and means-to-ends cross-culturally. Ends and means are interrelated intraculturally. Thirdly, reality is experienced through the symbolism of language and is defined and redefined by the ever-varied symbolisms of the many languages of mankind. Right and wrong, beautiful and ugly, normal and abnormal, and even the perception of time, distance, weight, and size are mediated by the conventions of any given group. Fourthly, a culture is not a closed system which rigidly molds the behavior of all members of a society. Culture, as such, Herskovits indicated, does nothing. It is simply the summation of the behavior and the habitual modes of thought of the persons who constitute a particular society at a given time. While these persons conform to the ways of the group, they vary somewhat in their reactions to the situations in which they find themselves. They vary, too, as whole societies, in the amount of change they desire. Herskovits asserted that "to recognize the values held to by a given people in no wise implies that they are a constant factor in the lives of succeeding generations of the same group" (*ibid.*, 64). Fifthly, each people, literate and nonliterate, feels that its own way of life is to be preferred to all others. Sixthly, a distinction is made between absolutes and universals. The cultural relativist knows of no absolute criteria of value or morals, but he does find values and morals, in differing forms, as universals in human culture. Finally, the principle of cultural relativism does not negate the codes that exist at a given time in a given culture.

Herskovits distinguished three aspects of cultural relativism: methodological, philosophical, and practical:

As method, relativism encompasses the principle of our science that, in studying a culture, one seeks to attain as great a degree of objectivity as possible; that one does not judge the modes of behavior one is describing, or seek to change them. Rather, one seeks to understand the sanctions of behavior in terms of the established relationships within the culture itself, and refrains from making interpretations that arise from a preconceived frame of reference. Relativism as philosophy concerns the nature of cultural values, and beyond this, the implications of an epistemology that derives from a recognition of the force of enculturative conditioning in shaping thought and behavior. Its practical aspects involve the application—the practice—of the philosophical principles derived from the method, to the wider, cross-cultural world scene. (1951b, 24)

Among the points made by Schmidt, a philosopher, in one of the best critiques of cultural relativism are the following:

(1) . . . the fact of cultural relativism is a true empirical statement with a mass of well-founded evidence behind it; (2) the thesis as a descriptive hypothesis may be true but the fact of cultural relativism is not evidence for the thesis; (3) neither the fact nor the thesis implies anything whatsoever concerning what is right or good because we cannot derive an "ought" from what "is"; (4) the fact and the thesis are compatible with diverse value theories; and (5) the thesis as a value theory must be rejected because its meaning implies its own refutation as a cross-cultural value theory. . . . (Schmidt, 1955, 788)

Schmidt argues that cultural relativists present a false dichotomy of value judgments that are either subjective and relative or transcendent and absolute. He says that a third alternative "maintains the objectivity of value judgments but rejects the source of such objectivity in some transcendent realm, locating it, rather, in the projection of human ideals" (*ibid.*, 790). In Schmidt's view, the relation of a judgment to a context does not destroy its objectivity. Such a value theory, he says, can admit the fact of cultural relativism, in fact, employ it fruitfully in the specification of the conditions surrounding a context in which a moral decision has to be made.[10] He criticizes Herskovits' "universals," saying that statements concerning the fact that every culture has some moral code, aesthetic preferences, and standard of truth are vague, and in addition are only descriptive, not prescriptive (*ibid.*, 790).

Quoting Herskovits' statement that "cultural relativism is a philosophy which, in recognizing the values set up by every society to guide its own life, lays stress on the dignity inherent in every body of custom, and on the need for tolerance of conventions though they differ from one's own," Hoebel says that Herskovits carries relativism beyond the acknowledgement of differences in cultural standards "to an implied dignity in all bodies of culture" (Hoebel, 1949, 473–74). To the admonition in behalf of tolerance based upon the recognition of "the validity of every set of norms for the people whose lives are guided by them, and the values these represent," Hoebel replies that a larger measure of tolerance is needed but that Herskovits fails to give due consideration to the fact that any society must select a few, and reject many, out of all the possible lines of behavior. Hoebel asserts also that "world society means a world culture with a certain measure of integration, and all present cultural systems are most certainly not compatible with each other. Some norms will have to give along the way. Not all can be tolerated" (*ibid.*, 474).

Differences in point of view concerning cultural relativism have not been resolved, but perhaps Herskovits' contributions to the discussion may be summarized as follows: (1) his emphasis on the

[10] For an illuminating comment on cultural relativism, with special reference to Herskovits' work, see Campbell (1973, v–xiii). Among other important points stressed by Campbell is the consistency of Herskovits' position on cultural relativism and his advocacy of cross-cultural comparison. Campbell asserts: ". . . He was not against quantitative multicultural comparison when the data from each culture were collected for that purpose by ethnographers who knew both the local culture and the purposes of the study. Under such conditions the possibility was created for the observations to be properly embedded in both the context of each local culture and the context of cross-cultural comparison" (*ibid.*, viii–ix).

fact of cultural relativism; (2) his stress on the importance of the method of cultural relativism in ethnological field work; (3) his furtherance of the study of values cross-culturally; (4) his stimulation of empirical investigations of relativism in realms other than that of values—in the total range of human thought and conduct, including perception and concepts of normal and pathological (1958c, 267–69); and (5) on the level of application, (a) his endorsement of the distinction between the curiosity function of social science—"pure science"—and the application of social scientific findings—engineering—and (b) his stress on "the importance of allowing, rather than imposing acceptances of cultural elements newly experienced" (1951b, 30).

The call of Herskovits and others for scientific objectivity in social scientific studies, and the admonition for tolerance concerning ways of life other than one's own, are still pertinent and important. In recent years, however, many social scientists have expressed strong interest in such additional concerns as how problems for scientific investigation are selected, defined, and funded; what uses are made of the data obtained in such investigations; and the responsibilities of social scientists for making their positions known on the critical social and political issues of their time.

Field Technique and Method. Prior to the middle 1960s, accounts of methods used by ethnologists in the field were rare.[11] From time to time, Herskovits offered a seminar in field methods; he would invite those who had returned from the field to talk about their experiences, and he would also give examples of his own procedures and discuss recording devices. In *Man and His Works* (1948b, ch. 6), Herskovits cited some examples of field technique from his experience in the late 1920s in Surinam, from Malinowski's work with the Trobriand Islanders a decade earlier, and from Evans-Pritchard's

[11] Two of the most useful books on ethnographic research thus far written appeared in 1970: Pertti J. Pelto, *Anthropological Research: The Structure of Inquiry*; and Morris Freilich, ed., *Marginal Natives: Anthropologists at Work*. The first covers all aspects of anthropological research; the second provides accounts by ten successful field researchers of adapting to a novel environment and solving a research problem. For the best analysis of the "insider-outsider" question, see Merton, 1972, 9–47.

research among the Azande and the Nuer in the 1930s. Concerning the doctrine of the "participant observer," the following rule was stated: "See as much as you can, participate whenever you are permitted to do so, and compound your experiences by discussing them formally and informally with natives as widely as you are able" (*ibid.*, 84). Herskovits enunciated other principles of field technique that are now commonplace: the use of a wide range of persons as informants—the young as well as the elders, men and women, priests, initiates, and lay persons; and checking information for omissions, distortions, or untruths. References were made to the genealogical method; village mapping; the use of the native language, "pidgin" dialects, and the interpreter; and biographies and autobiographies as tools. Above all, Herskovits stressed honesty of purpose and sensitivity (*ibid.*, 93).

In 1950, Herskovits described an ethnographic field technique which he called "the hypothetical situation." Developed in Liberia, Dahomey, Trinidad, and Brazil, it consisted of "devising, *ad hoc*, situations in the life of a people in terms of hypothetical persons, relationships, and events, which, being in accord with the prevalent patterns of the culture, are used to direct and give form to discussions with informants and other members of a group being studied (1950, 32)." This technique had proved to be especially useful in discussions of situations involving the intervention of supernatural power, but it was employed in probing other elements of culture of which the members of the society were reluctant to speak. In Haiti, for example, he reported that "many discussions of the *vodun* cult were begun, at least, by introducing hypothetical situations as if they were merely in the realm of possible happenings." In the functioning of this "creative projective mechanism," the hypothetical person often turned out to be the informant himself, freed by this approach to reveal aspects of his personality that he would try to conceal in speaking of himself. Likewise, he may speak of happenings to others that he might be hesitant to reveal if he were naming "actual" persons. Both in the personal and the cultural sense, Herskovits said, an informant can and will go farther in expressing reactions than would otherwise be the case.

In 1954, Herskovits discussed the problems in ethnographic field research that had received most attention up to that time: duration, communication, rapport, comparison, and historic depth (1954, 3–24). He restated the principal reason for the abandonment of the classical comparative approach, namely, "a realization of the heterogeneous nature of the data employed and the disregard for cultural context that characterized their use" (*ibid.*, 18–19). Also reiterated here was his point that acculturation studies start with established historical contacts and analyze the cultural reorientations that can be observed. In the ethnohistorical approach, the nature and intensity of cultural changes are explained by ethnographic data welded to information obtained from historical documents. Other questions discussed in this paper were the utility of sampling to supplement the intensive study of a single group in the total society, restudies of a given people, and the comparison of the findings of independent observers among neighboring peoples.

Returning to the question of ethnographic comparison in 1956, Herskovits first asked the question: What are we comparing?

Are we concerned with items of culture, perhaps in the tradition of the classical 'comparative method'? Are we comparing cultural institutions, as in studies of totemism, or the market, or magical practices? Do we wish to draw comparisons between whole cultural aspects, as in general treatises on art, or social organization, or economics, or folklore? Or, as in the case of those concerned, for example, with national character, do we take a holistic approach and attempt to compare total cultures? Again, we may ask what we hope to achieve through our comparisons. Do we wish to establish the boundaries of cultural variation, so as to assess these in terms of limiting biopsychic and ecological factors? Or in philosophical terms, are we seeking to discern the universals in human behavior that give mankind a common basis for the differentials in perceptive and value patterns that guide action in each society? Are we attempting to establish contacts between peoples, and analyze the historical implications of these contacts? Is our aim to understand the dynamic processes which underlie cultural change? Moving to the methodological plane, we ask how we go about

Life and Work

making our comparisons. Here classification is of the essence. Shall we draw our comparisons in terms of a particular phenomenon, or by historic stream, or by area? (1956, 135)

Herskovits' main interest in the method of comparison was in comparisons by historic stream, especially in the field of Afroamerican studies. He gave four reasons for the minimal attention given Afroamerican contributions in comparative analyses that had appeared up to the middle 1950s: (1) many anthropologists still regarded anthropology as the study of "primitive" peoples, but in Afroamerican societies the African customs that remain are permeated with reinterpreted innovations; (2) its geographical definition cannot be delimited in customary anthropological terms—it lies in both the Americanist and the Africanist fields, but in the usual sense in neither; (3) Afroamerican societies do not stand alone, clearly apart, as do the tribal groups ordinarily studied by anthropologists; and (4) in Afroamerican studies, as against the then-prevailing pattern of research interests in anthropology, it is necessary to take into account the dominant orientations in Afroamerican cultures—belief systems, folklore, and music. Herskovits referred to his use of the method of comparison in the field of Afroamerican studies, including the concept of the degree of retention of Africanisms in different aspects of culture and in different regions of a geographical area, as well as the differences in intensity according to the socioeconomic position of the individual; the introduction of a corrective to the dichotomies often drawn between fragmentation and integration in the study of culture; and the concepts of syncretism, reinterpretation, and cultural focus. In short, Herskovits developed a set of concepts to explain why, in a situation where the representatives of two or more peoples are in continuous contact, some traditional elements of the cultures are retained virtually unchanged, while others are combined in varying ways with innovations, and why some innovations are rejected.

PART II

Selections from the Writings of Melville J. Herskovits

With the exception of Dahomey: An Ancient West African Kingdom, (2 vols., New York, J. J. Augustin, 1938), all of the published monographs and books of Melville J. Herskovits are still in print, some of them in paperback editions. Most of the selections from his publications that are included here are not readily available to students and to the general public. They give us some idea of the man and his contributions to anthropology. All selections have been reprinted with the permission of the publishers. Some of the selections have been abridged.

In their field work and writings, Melville and Frances Herskovits manifested a strong interest in all of the arts. The first two selections are parts of their portrayal of the traditional graphic and plastic art forms of Dahomey. These reports were published in 1934, a time when few studies of African art had been made. (See also the section on Plastic and Graphic Arts in chapter 4.)

I The Art of Dahomey*

I BRASS-CASTING AND APPLIQUÉ CLOTHS

✤ Brass is regarded as a precious metal in Dahomey. During the native régime, it had the same value—appreciatively, if not in terms of European exchange—as gold, and among the mass of people this evaluation still holds, for its possession remains a luxury of ruling chiefs and men of wealth. In the days of the kings, the brass-workers, who occasionally also used silver as a medium, were the court jewelers. They formed a closed guild, and their work was localized in Abomey. They wrought their wares within narrow traditional bounds in all that concerned cult-objects, but in the secular products of their art, free reign was given them to create whatever they felt would please the monarch and those of his favorites who helped shape the monarch's reactions.

The technique of casting employed is the *cire-perdue* method. Each figure is modeled in beeswax and enclosed in a clay mold. The mold, after being dried in the sun, is placed inside the furnace until the wax is melted. Next the brass (or silver) is foundered and, when liquid, is poured inside the mold. When this has cooled the mold is broken and the piece is ready for tooling and polishing. In those pieces, like that of the hunter and dog, where several units are involved, each is modeled separately and has its own mold. When cast and tooled, the various units are soldered together. If two identical pieces are required—and for some obscure reason, possibly because twins are sacred in Dahomey, most brass objects are produced in pairs—two separate molds are made and destroyed. With but rare exceptions, such as the wide bracelets and armlets worn by the women who dance for the royal ancestors, and the ceremonial axes used by the Thunder priests in their rituals, brass objects are treated in the round, and the figures are representations of animal and human forms. In earlier times the emphasis was on animal representations, partly because the brass figures, which were intended for

* REPRINTED FROM *The American Magazine of Art*, 27, no. 2 (February 1934): 67–76. (Written with Frances Herskovits.)

use in the worship of the Ancestors, depicted totem animals. More particularly, however, the animal figures symbolized the monarchs themselves, for the lion represents one king, the buffalo another, and the elephant a third, and all objects upon which such emblems appear are associated with these kings.

The human forms enter chiefly into the secular art, their use being merely to provide objects of display which, in the house of a man of position, makes beautiful his dwelling and validates by these symbols of affluence the importance of the place he holds. Tradition tells that the more recent kings had a great storehouse filled with brass figures, and that all emissaries to the Dahomean court were brought to this storehouse that they might report to their countrymen the fabulous wealth of Dahomey. Each emissary who thus viewed this vast collection of prized objects was made a gift of several of them to take back to his king, since, of all the neighboring kingdoms, Dahomey alone produced these figures—something that is true to this day. Another tradition explains why, in earlier days, human reproductions were frowned upon. The tale recounts that long ago the human form was freely used on calabash decorations and all other types of decorative objects. Then it came to pass that fewer and fewer children were born in the land. A diviner was summoned who, by consulting Fate, discovered that the gods held that men had to make their choice between creating their "offspring" on calabash surfaces, or having living children.

Yet another tradition touches upon the point we have raised, whether brass-work can be viewed as an indigenous art, inasmuch as before European goods were made available to the Africans, no brass existed in Dahomey. "Brass," says the Dahomean, "is a white man's thing, but it came to Dahomey long ago. Before there was brass there was iron, and our ancestors knew how to get rock from the mountainside and turn it into iron. From iron many objects were made." Many ceremonial objects of an artistic order are still made of iron— the representation of the snake, and musical gongs; while at a shrine in Allada, where all the Dahomean kings came to be crowned, we were shown a beautifully wrought iron bell with a human head topping its long handle, and the legs and arms of the stylized human

107

Melville J. Herskovits

figure, spider-like in thinness, extending outward from the central motif, a piece said to date from the first king of Dahomey.

Among the crafts which rank high in the view of the Dahomeans is that of the workers in cloth. "Thanks to these men," said several, "our gods are finely clothed."

What are the implications of this statement, when considered in terms of Dahomean life? The gods—and there are many of them—are worshipped by dancing, and for these dances each cult-devotee wears a special costume according to the god to whom he is vowed. For the Thunder deities, for example, part of the costume consists of a short skirt, full as a ballet skirt, which is decorated with designs in appliqué symbolizing the various attributes of the divinity. Or, in the worship of the Ancestors, the "Amazons," as they sing their songs glorifying the deeds of the dead kings, wear short tightly belted dresses, and these have appliqué designs sewed on the plain white cloth of which they are made.

Yet the use of appliqué designs goes into many more aspects of Dahomean life than just the religious phases. Thus, the highest insignia of office in Africa is the umbrella, and in Dahomey these umbrellas, often multicolored, are decorated with appliqué designs on the long lappets. The state umbrellas of the kings were of great size, and all of them were richly covered with such designs. Not alone the king but princes and men of lower rank had their umbrellas, as did many of the religious culthouses, and all were characterized by these designs in appliqué. The rituals of death in Dahomey are very complex and involve great expense to those who participate. One reason for the costliness of participation is that the dead must be equipped with cloths to insure for him a proper status in the eternity of the ancestral generations. A man's best friend—and friendship, too, is institutionalized in Dahomey, requiring specific gifts upon death—supplies in addition to the ritual burial cloth of native weave, several others, and one is a man's cloth on which appliqué designs are sewed. Each group of designs is a proverb, and as he presents the cloth and displays it before the mourners, he speaks these proverbs which, by the use of hyperbole, dwell on the qualities of the dead and the depth of the friendship between the two men. When so-

108

cieties of a social character are formed, each of them acquires a flag that consists of a series of appliqué designs sewed on cloth, usually white, recounting the callings and exploits of the members. These, however, are by no means all of the uses for appliqué designs. We see them on the caps and bonnets worn by the chiefs, on the awning-like tops of their hammocks, and, above all, we see them on cloths that have no utilitarian value at all but, like paintings and tapestries in our own culture, are regarded as works of art and are made to hang upon the walls of those who can afford them.

Though occasionally black designs are sewn on a white surface, the favorite background is either gold or black, and the other colors used are red, blue, green, and white. When the background is black the principal figure is done in gold, and when gold, in black. Human figures may be either black or red, for the skin-color of the Dahomean is distinctly of a reddish tinge, rather than the deep brownish-black usually associated with Negro peoples. The material used is sateen for the colors, cambric for the white, while small units of a design are often done in a brocaded sateen. Patterns are made on stiff paper for each design-unit, and these patterns are kept from one generation to the next. When a new cloth is being planned, several of these units can be arranged and rearranged in the sand until a pleasing composition is obtained, but if entirely new figures are to be introduced it is possible to draw the projected composition in the sand and then play with the grouping of the several figures or emblems until the artist is satisfied with the effect. Once this is attained, he proceeds to cut out his patterns.

Yet even though these patterns are kept and inherited—we know of one instance, at least, where these exist four generations back—it must not be assumed that, except for certain traditional renderings, this art exhibits the static quality usually attributed to primitive art. Let us take, as a case in point, a design which depicts a man who is being done to death by a lion, and the hunters who come to his rescue. . . . The first picture has as its central figure a lion, with an antelope, not a human being, in its mouth, while two men, one above the lion and one below him, aim their clubs at him. This design was made by the grandfather of the man who is at present chief of the cloth-workers' guild. In the second cloth of the series, the lion, always the central figure, is also being attacked by two men. They are in the same position in relation to the animal, but in their hands are bows and arrows. This, the first revision, was done by the father of the present chief. In the third cloth, the lion has seized the hand of a man, and his claws are fastened in the back of his victim. A hunter, with gun and knife, is coming to the rescue; the human figure above the lion has been omitted from the design. This cloth was designed by the present chief, who expressed his criticism of the earlier compositions in explaining his own. The last cloth of the series, designed by the son who will succeed this chief, shows the lion with a firm grip on his victim. Here there are three human figures: the victim and two rescuers. One of these holds the lion's tail and is about to strike him with a hunting knife, while, from below, the third has his gun trained upon the animal ready to shoot. In each instance the changes were made to heighten the dramatic effect and, also, since the legend that has inspired these four cloths demands that the lion be overpowered, so to depict the scene as to give the conviction that the man will triumph.

In comparing the treatment of human and animal figures in brass and cloth, it is at once evident that they represent different traditions. The simple explanation of this, to one unacquainted with Dahomean culture, is that the technical problem of representing figures on a two-dimensional surface was met in one way, and that of the three-dimensional modeling in another. The fact, however, is that while the brass pieces represent an independent tradition, the appliqué cloth-work is strictly derivative, being patterned after the bas-reliefs modeled on the compound walls of king and nobles and after the paintings found on the walls of the temples to the gods.[1] This does not mean that the cloths represent a slavish copying of the bas-reliefs, for new compositions in appliqué cloth are con-

[1] The bas-reliefs on the walls of the palace of the kings at Abomey have been reproduced in color in the definitive work on these figures by E. G. Waterlot, *Les Bas-Reliefs des Batiments royaux d'Abomey* (Paris, 1926). For those to whom this work is not available, a discussion of these reliefs and reproductions from it are contained in a review of this work by M. J. Herskovits in *The Arts*, 13 (1928):128–30.

stantly appearing. Moreover, although both brasses and cloths are strictly representational in intent—there are relatively few symbolic art-forms in Dahomey—the stylization employed for each medium is distinct, and follows rules that are well understood by those who create in each medium. Thus it is, in Dahomean art as in any other, that the Dahomean artist, no less than the European, works in approved media according to approved rules of style and composition. Yet in Dahomey, as in Europe, the artist is ever the individualist, ever the creator. The media he employs, the traditions which unconsciously direct his work, act only as limits beyond which, however great his genius, he rarely goes.

2 The Art of Dahomey *

II WOOD CARVING

✥ While, as had been noted in our preceding discussion, work in brass and appliqué cloth represented the aristocratic arts, under control of the reigning native officialdom wood carving afforded, as it still affords, the primary artistic outlet for the Dahomean populace. This observation, however, is to be qualified in several ways. To begin with, it is only the male portion of the populace to whom is granted this opportunity for self-expression, for women may not work in wood either in Dahomey or elsewhere in West Africa. Again, though all men may carve, and many men do at least carve the small human figures which they wear as personal charms, there are not many singularly fine carvers. In pre-conquest days the outstanding carvers were summoned to the capital and commanded to work for the king, or, if their reputations had not reached the ears of the king's courtiers, then the local chief exercised his prerogative of command, and used the carver to make stools, wands of office, and images for shrines, or charms for himself and the villages that he ruled. Carvers of excellence were also called to work for the priests, and for the temples of the gods.

Unlike brass, silver, and cloth work, however, which are distinct

* Reprinted from *The American Magazine of Art* vol. 27, no. 3 (March 1934): 124–31. (Written with Frances Herskovits.)

luxuries, wood carving is a necessity of the humblest household. In a country where caste was maintained by restricting the wearing of sandals at the royal court, for example, to the king only, or to the ranking member of a group of chiefs when these were gathered together, the use of carved figures was denied to none. The explanation for this lies in the fact that these carvings are an integral part of the religious life of the people, and that freedom to worship the gods was not denied even to slaves.

What are these carvings that are among the essentials of Dahomean life? Every compound has somewhere near its entrance a shrine to Legba, the divine trickster and the intermediary between men and gods. Under the low-roofed shrine to Legba is an image intended for the god himself, to animate at his pleasure. This must be modeled in clay, but the images of one or sometimes two of the wives of this god are of wood. Directly before the entrance to the compound a magic charm to ward off evil is always to be seen, and this most commonly consists of a wooden image, which may be Janus-faced, or may be a single figure facing sternly outward or with its gaze fastened on the compound itself. At the side of individual houses within the compound, or inside the houses, to one side of the doorway, or one at each side of the doorway, as sentinels, are other figures carved in wood, magically treated and empowered by a maker of charms with supernatural strength drawn from a given deity. Nor are these all. We have already mentioned the small personal charms, wooden images ranging from three to five inches in height, which a man prefers to carve for himself, so that no strange carver may knowingly or unwittingly introduce an element to invalidate the powers to be given it. In addition, any special venture, or a quarrel, may introduce into the household other magic preventives and some of these may be asked to reside inside images of wood. Then there is the cult of Destiny. At least one adult male within every compound will have ascertained, through the diviner, his personal Destiny, and all undertakings which hold the threat of danger to the physical or material well-being of the inhabitants of that compound will be referred to a diviner who will interpret the questions put to him in terms of the relation of this man's personal Destiny to the Universal Destiny. To do this, objects necessary for divining are called into play. One of these objects is a cup for the palm-kernels used for divining, always finely carved if the means of the consultant, or his personal artistic gifts, permit of such a possession. Another is a carved stick, eight or ten inches long, with which to call Fate, and this is supplemented by a second stick, also carved, ending in a wooden bell, which has similar use. Finally there is the board on which the diviner makes his lines as he throws his kernels. This is edged with a carved border figuring the symbols of the cult, and is always worked with consummate artistry.

Even the poorest households have carved objects such as have been enumerated. Families of position also possess the means which permit them to have carvings made on the low benches for men and women, and, if there is a chief in the family, his "recade," or wand of office, will bear a carved totemic, or proverbially symbolic animal to serve as a handle to swing over one shoulder. Those of high rank carry walking sticks with carved handles, and their stools are raised on the heads of two, four, or eight carved bearers standing on a base, the whole carved from a single block of wood. Shrines and temples to the gods, as well as shrines for the patron deities of diviners, or makers of charms, or workers of black magic, all have one or more images to symbolize an ancestor who initiated the worship of the gods, or the cult of divining, or the knowledge of good and bad magic.

And to all these must be added the small twin figures. Twins are sacred both in Dahomey and Western Nigeria. If one of a pair of twins dies, the living child must carry about with it an image to represent the dead twin, and when the living child eats, he shares of every dish that he partakes with the image of his dead twin. Or, if a gift is given the living child, part of it must be offered to the image. The cult of twins is too complex in its symbolic ramifications to detail here; it is sufficient to indicate that this is done because twins share one soul, and if the dead were made envious, it would kill the living child. The use of the images for twins is more prevalent in Nigeria than in Dahomey. There, when both twins die, two images are made, and these are placed on a mound of earth and are worshipped.

As we sketched briefly the uses to which wood carvings are put, we made the repeated observation that this type of carving and that is wrought with artistic excellence. Here several questions come to mind. Is that excellence apparent to the Dahomean and the Nigerian himself? Is the native worker aware of what he creates, of the effects he is trying to achieve? Has he standards? Is he critical of his own work? Of the work of others? And is he subject to the criticism of those who will see his carvings? A motion picture record of artists and craftsmen at work, taken only incidentally to study techniques, but primarily to register the motor behavior of these people for the purpose of contrasting it with similar records of the motor behavior of Negro peoples in the New World, throws objective light on some of these questions. We shall now at this point endeavor to abstract that record in words.

The African wood carver fashions his pieces with the aid of tools produced by native iron workers. In Dahomey the carvers whom we saw at work used only a small adze, a chisel, and a knife the size of a pocketknife; indeed, one of the carvers had replaced the native knife with a European pocketknife. With the chisel the piece is roughly blocked out—head, neck, arms, breasts if the figure is that of a woman, legs—the handle of the adze being used as a hammer to give force to the bite of the chisel's blade. This done, the carver takes up the piece in his left hand, and with adze in the right, sharpens the outlines of the figure he has blocked out. As he does this, he frequently pauses and holds the figure away from him, looking intently at the proportions of torso and head and extremities. His strokes are firm, but unhurried, and as he proceeds, the pauses to examine what he has done recur more frequently. When his adzing has progressed to a point where the figure is fully outlined and needs finer treatment, the small knife is brought into play, rounding and smoothing the curves of the figure, and working in the details of face and body—fashioning ears and eyes and nostrils, fingers and toes. This accomplished, a final polishing of the figure is necessary. This is sometimes done with the use of sand, but more often with a leaf whose surface is rough and spiny, and leaves the wood with little trace of the lines left by adze and knife.

The figure thus completed still has none of the patination that is associated with African art. Its color is pale brown or light red, for though hard woods are almost always used, the color of many varieties of these African woods is light. It is only after offerings of blood and corn meal, and more particularly, of palm oil, are given the statuette that it slowly turns the dark, rich color that characterizes the pieces which we figure here. Or, in the case of smaller figures, it is only after years of handling that the patination comes.

Not all of the gifted carvers make wood-working their profession. But, as is true of all the crafts in Dahomey, professional wood carving is carried on by the same families generation after generation, thus establishing regional traditions. Each of these regional traditions in reality represents a school founded by a remote ancestor, and though significant variants often occur, as they must when creative artists translate a tradition in terms of their own personalities, the work of each school is nevertheless distinctive, and the carvings of its members are recognizable by the Dahomean as deriving from it. A close study of the figures . . . will show a difference in treatment of the ear, for example, that is clearly traceable to such groups of carvers. Or there are the matters of bodily proportions, of the modeling of the torso, of the attempts at introducing realistic detail, or of achieving portraiture. Not all pieces executed by a given "school" are, of course, of equal artistic quality. There is always one man whom the gods will favor above the others; his pieces will be in greatest demand. He will work longest without tiring, and the gods will relish coming to dwell in his images. Such a man may, in order not to give cause for envy to those who have evil powers at their command, fashion an indifferently good image to represent the wife of Legba in the shrine before his compound, but on the images for the personal charms of his family, which are not in public view, he will lavish all the artistry at his command. Or, it may be that his zeal

115

for adding to his earnings may cause him to meet his family and personal needs for these images carelessly.

The Dahomean view of the carver, however, is that he seldom has the prudence to amass any wealth by his work—a very reprehensible fault, indeed, in the light of generally accepted native values. He is, they say, always eager to go off into the bush in search of fine wood, and once gone, he may not return for weeks. Upon his return, he will busy himself making a figure from some piece of rare wood, working long and contentedly, and neglect to make a mortar, or a stool for which a buyer is waiting. That is why, say the Dahomeans, wood carvers are poor providers for their wives and children. In the days of the kings they were no less dilatory, so that when a monarch wished one of these famous carvers to make certain objects for him, he would send out a detachment of soldiers to bring him to the palace, where he was kept under guard until he finished his task. "The king could have had him killed for not obeying him, but that wouldn't have got him the carvings. . . . And they were all like that, these carvers." Thus, whether the artistic temperament is universal or not, it would seem that in Dahomey, at least, the wood carvers manifest temperament.

The gifted professional carver, then, is viewed as an unworldly fellow, under the spell of the bush that yields him his wood, and the figures which he models from it. What of the amateur, the man who makes his own image, for charms, not because he fears the magic of the maker of these images, or because he has not the means with which to buy them, but who, because of an inner drive, works steadily and with intensity on such figures whenever he has the leisure? If he is a man of position, he will do this in the greatest secrecy, it is true, but do it he will. The reason for the secrecy lies in the logic of Dahomean values, for a carver is a worker, and a worker is at the command of those who have need of his labor. Once a man becomes the head of a group of prosperous households, he is the one who commands, and to place himself in a position to take orders from anyone would be to demean himself. This, in turn, would mean that not alone the living members of the family would feel the humiliation, but the dead members would resent the lowering of his status, and would punish him with those means the dead have at their command. . . .

Herskovits' field work in Africa in 1931 resulted in the publication of one of his major works, Dahomey: An Ancient West African Kingdom. *Because cooperative endeavors are intrinsically interesting, and because of the links Herskovits found between mutual aid in West Africa and in New World Negro cultures, we reproduce here parts of his discussion of the cooperative element in Dahomean life. (See also the section on Technology and Economic Life in chapter 3.)*

Herskovits thought that the Dahomean love of organization is best seen in the numerous associations for mutual self-help. Young men predominate in the dokpwe, *the basic cooperative group, but the elderly members of a village perform such tasks as their capability permits. Because of the singing, the feasting, and the competition, the work of the* dokpwe *is regarded as recreation rather than arduous labor. The* dokpwe *helps everyone, chief and poor man. One chief said: "If you need a house, it will build one for you; if you have a field to cultivate, it will break your ground. When you are sick, it helps you; when you die, it buries you." Each* dokpwe *is headed by a hereditary chief and his three assistants (1938b, 1:63–70).*

3   The Cooperative Element in Dahomean Life*

✤ The functions of the *dokpwe* during funerals will be considered in the later chapters dealing with death, and only its economic aspects will be treated here. First of all, it may be summoned to render mutual aid to its members. The case of a villager who is ill, or who

* Reprinted from Melville J. Herskovits, *Dahomey: An Ancient West African Kingdom* (New York: J. J. Augustin, 1938), 1:71–77.

is too old to do the hard work of preparing his field for planting and has no one to call on to aid him, may be considered. In such an instance the *dokpwe* is assembled by the *dokpwega* [chief] to break the ground for the one who is incapacitated, so that planting may be done and the man will not lack food that year. If the owner of such a field is poor, neither the nominal fee for the *dokpwega* nor food for the *dokpwe* is exacted. He will, of course, have participated in the work of the *dokpwe* during the earlier years of his life, or, if he happened to be a young man and ill, he would expect to continue this cooperation. In this sense, therefore, the *dokpwe* is to be regarded as an organization which insures to each member the cultivation of his fields, even though he himself may be incapacitated.

A second type of cooperative activity engaged in by the *dokpwe* is exemplified in the case of a man whose fields are too extensive to permit them to be hoed by his own labor and the labor of those whose service he has at his disposal. Such a man may summon the *dokpwe* to help clear his fields, but for him the work is not done altogether free of cost, though the amount the owner of the fields must expend is small in comparison with the labor involved. When such a man wishes to call the *dokpwe*, he goes to the *dokpwega* with a bottle of spirits, four yards of cloth, and two francs fifty centimes, which is divided between the *dokpwega* and his sub-chiefs. The *legede* [assistant chief] is then instructed to notify the members of the *dokpwe* that at the time agreed upon, they are to gather at the appointed place to do this work. It is incumbent upon the owner of the field, however, to provide a feast, and for this he slaughters a goat or a pig, and provides as rich and varied fare as he can afford. This meal is the only recompense the individual member of the *dokpwe* receives.

A *dokpwe* is also called upon to aid men fulfil the duties they owe the parents of their wives. The system, known as *asitogle*, renders it mandatory for a son-in-law to perform a major piece of work once every year or two for his father-in-law, and to keep the house of his wife's mother in good repair. To neglect these duties entails a serious breach, and should a son-in-law fail without good cause to discharge these obligations, his tardiness will first be called to his attention by his father-in-law, while if he persists in ignoring these duties over a period of years, his wife will be taken away to the home of her parents and will eventually be divorced from him. It is not usual for such tasks to be neglected, however, and for the man with numerous wives, whose total amount of work owed his various parents-in-law is far beyond the power of any one individual, the institution of the *dokpwe* makes it possible for the *asitogle* system to exist. When a son-in-law has arranged for a *dokpwe* to do work of this category, he requests of his father-in-law to be allowed to perform some task for him. This request is couched in terms which reflect the code of understatement that the relationship of inferior to superior in Dahomey demands, for he says to the older man, "May I be permitted to do some slight piece of work for you in three or four days?" When the wife's father asks for details, the reply is, "I have ordered some thirty or forty men to come and work in your fields," or "I have arranged for thirty or forty men to build the wall you have been wanting built," or "I have asked sixty men to come to thatch the roof of your new house." It is evident, therefore, why it is said "A man who has many daughters is a rich man."

Yet the inference must not be drawn that a man does not desire sons as well as daughters, nor that sons do not help increase the patrimony, for a son works for his father until the age of twenty or twenty-five. Before a man establishes his own household, however, he does have his own fields, and this establishes a fourth category where the *dokpwe* functions. A son who has his own fields, but who must still serve his father, will request the *dokpwega* to summon the *dokpwe* to do his required work for him. If he has sufficient means, he will pay; if not, the villagers will do this work for him under the direction of their chief without any cost to him, except his obligation to do the same for them when he is summoned by the *dokpwega*. Even when a man has passed the age when he is under the direct control of his father, he does not necessarily put aside these earlier obligations, but as a courtesy to his parent may send a "little *dokpwe*" of perhaps fifteen or twenty men to work his father's fields.[1]

1 This deference to the old, or to those of superior position in the family, is fundamental in Dahomean usage and is reflected in all types of behavior as,

Once a date is settled upon with the *dokpwega*, the members of a *dokpwe* who are to perform a given task assemble at the place named by the *legede*, and set out together for the field where the hoeing is to be done, or for the compound where the wall is to be erected or the house to be thatched. They are led by a flutist whose shrill notes they can easily follow, for the distance is often great and perhaps not known to some of them.[2] They have drums, gongs, and rattles, and use these to accompany the songs they sing. If the one who has summoned them is a man of large means, they may find upon arriving at their destination that other *dokpwe* are at work. This gives added zest to the occasion, for it allows competition in the work. If a field is to be hoed, each *dokpwe* strives against the others to see which can first finish its allotted portion. If the task is to thatch a roof, each *dokpwe*, if there are two, takes a side and, in each stage of construction tries to be first to reach the ridge-pole. The reward for those who are quickest is the privilege of singing songs of derision against the opposing *dokpwe* until the laggards have caught up with the winners. This desire for competitive struggle goes so far that if only one *dokpwe* is present, it will be divided, one-half of the members competing against the other half. What is accomplished by a *dokpwe* bulks large, but the labor of any one individual is not arduous. The work may involve the expenditure of much muscular energy, it is true, but what a man does as *dokpwe* is performed to the accompaniment of the rhythms of the *dokpwe* work-songs, while the fact that his fellows are watching him is a never-failing drive. Then, too, no one individual works for too long a stretch, for one man relieves the next who, while he rests, joins in the singing before he again takes his place. To climax the occasion is the feast, where quantities of relished food, which the day's sponsor of the work provides as plentifully as he is able, are spread before the workers. For no small measure of

---

for example, where a mature man of position will sit on the floor instead of on a stool when in the presence of his father or of an elder brother who has inherited the headship of his family.

[2] In the case of one *dokpwe* observed building a compound-wall in Abomey, the men, accompanied by the girls of their village, had come from a distance of forty-five kilometers, where the village in which the son-in-law of the compound head had his residence was located.

social prestige accrues to him who gives with an open hand, gaining as he does the reputation of having the means with which to provide bountifully. . . . Cooperative work is not confined to the performance of the types of work which appertain peculiarly to the *dokpwe*, however. The practice among the iron-workers, for example, is for one smith to buy a quantity of scrap iron and keep it until such time as it is his turn to benefit from the labor of his fellows, for whom he has been working in the meantime. When this time arrives, all the members of the forge convert the iron he has acquired into hoes, axes, bush-knives, and other salable goods. The owner of the iron then is free to sell these implements, and to keep the proceeds gained from selling them. This money he will use for living expenses and the purchase of scrap iron, meanwhile working for his associates, until it is once more his turn to have the use of the combined labor-power of his forge. One of their number is chosen as leader and arbiter and in this manner the work goes on without undue friction. Cooperative work of this sort is usually done by groups of persons who belong to the same sib and extended family. This fact, that the members of a forge are relatives, is accounted for in tradition by a tale which tells how one of the early kings directed several families—twenty men, twenty women—to become iron-workers, and how the descendants of these matings carry on the craft.

Among the weavers cooperative effort also obtains, the whole group working on the material of first one and then the other of the members, so that each member in turn becomes the owner of a large supply of cloths. The cloth workers live and work together and strict discipline prevails among them. It is said that only three groups of weavers are to be found in the whole of Dahomey, all of them in Abomey. The weavers, like the iron-workers, are related.[3] A chief, who heads the principal group, controls all the weavers. The designs are restricted, and a member of the guild must have permission of the chief to reproduce and sell a cloth of a given design, and must pay

[3] The fact that weavers are only found in Abomey was not verified, though none were seen elsewhere in Dahomey. In view of the extent to which cloths of European manufacture are worn, it would be quite possible that a relatively small group could today supply the entire demand for their product.

for the use of a pattern not invented by himself. An example of the control which is exercised in this group was witnesed when one of the cloth workers sold without authorization one of the products of his loom. Great objection was voiced by the other members of the guild, and it was said at the time that this man would be fined for his offense. This same organization and discipline characterizes the groups of workers who appliqué designs on cloth, except in their case the conception of designs as an individual matter is more emphasized, and the ownership of these patterns is more jealously observed.

Pottery is fired and often marketed cooperatively. A woman who does not get on with the others of her group, particularly if she cuts her prices, is punished not only by having her stock of pottery broken by her associates, but also by being forced to work for a time without remuneration before she is readmitted to all the privileges of the guild.

One may say, indeed, that this principle of cooperative work is to be found in all phases of Dahomean economic life. Yet exceptions are had in the instance of the jewelers and wood-carvers, who are regarded as artists rather than artisans. While men who follow these callings may perhaps work together—in the case of the jewelers, the forges are grouped much as those of the iron-workers—they are not subject to control as to the time they work, what they produce, how they sell their handiwork, or what prices they obtain for them. A man's creations are his own and he neither takes kindly to direction nor works without manifesting jealousy toward the products of others.

The wood-carver is even more of an individualist than the jeweler, and in consequence is not esteemed a dependable individual; the women say that marriage to one of them affords a precarious existence, for these carvers do not bend their energies to providing well for their families. There are very few professional wood-carvers, most of the carving being produced outside the economic field—carvings that are not sold, but made for the pleasure of the carver and either used by him or given as gifts. Considered from the point of view of Dahomean economics, then, wood-carving is only of minor importance. It

is significant, however, in that it offers an example of individualism
in a society so highly organized as is that of Dahomey.

In traditional Dahomean belief, human beings possess
more than one "soul." The generic term for soul is se, and when a
man dies Mawu (a female deity of the Sky pantheon) uses the body
as clay for shaping other bodies. The first of the multiple souls
which all persons have is the soul inherited from an ancestor, in effect, his "guardian spirit." The second soul is made from the earth
that has been gathered and shaped into the form in which the person is to appear on earth—his personal soul. The third soul is the
great se, "the Mawu who lives in every person's body." In western
world concepts, these three souls correspond roughly with the individual's biological nature, his personality, and his intellect and in-
tuition. When a man dies, his second soul dies with him. Herskovits
reported that the third soul was "held to be the soul that at death
returns to bear witness against the semedo (second soul) if the latter
attempts to falsify the record of the conduct on earth of the human
body both souls actuated in life." Some individuals in Dahomey
could claim a fourth soul. These individuals were adult males who
had had their complete Fa (Destiny) revealed. This fourth soul concerned itself with the collective destiny of the individual's entire
household, including, in earlier times, his slaves (1938b, 2:231-38).
Herskovits' account of the multiple-soul concept in Dahomey is of
special interest because of the reinterpretation of this belief among
some New World Negroes (see the section on Religion and Related
Aspects of Culture in chapter 3).

Melville J. Herskovits

4 The World of the Dead in Dahomean Belief*

✤ What, then, are the beliefs concerning the world of the dead?
The dead reside in the sky, say many, and not in the earth. "If you
dig in the earth, what do you find? Earth, and stones, and more earth,
and sometimes wealth—minerals, and precious stones out of which
beads are made. It may be that you will find the bones of those who
died long ago. But no matter how much you dig you will find nothing
in the earth but earth." That there is no unanimity concerning the
location of this world of the dead, however, is evidenced by folktales
in the "orphan-child" cycle, where a girl who has lost her mother is
mistreated by the other wives of her father and, weeping, goes to
her mother's grave to tell of her plight. The mother soon appears
before her and, in most variants, directs her to the "market of the
dead," which is either actually on earth or underground.

The path to the other world, however, is well enough understood
to allow its being diagrammed. The definitive funeral over, the soul
of the dead, after taking a long path, comes to a river known as the
Azile. This river is guarded by a watchman who demands money to
ferry the departing soul and his burdens across. Some time later he
comes to another river called Gudu. This boatman demands tobacco
before he will permit the dead soul to reach the other side. Next a
steep mountain must be climbed, but when the toilsome journey up
its slope has been achieved, a third guardian of the path halts the
soul and demands cloths for his toll. On descending the other side
of the mountain, a final river called Selu bars his way. Here, however,
neither gifts nor money prevail; he can only be ferried if the boatman
is called by the living who have been left behind. It is for this reason
that the final ceremonies of the *tovodu* rites must be so meticulously
carried out, for should this not be done, the ghosts would be doomed
to wander between the worlds, and wandering restlessly, would become evil spirits, wreaking their vengeance on their neglectful children. Once arrived in the land of the dead, however, the soul of the

* Reprinted from Melville J. Herskovits, *Dahomey, An Ancient West African Kingdom* (New York: J. J. Augustin, 1938), 2:239–44.

124

recently dead person is welcomed by those of his own family who are already there, who ask him for news of the world of the living, and who are given the gifts and messages that have been sent by the living at the time of his funeral. He takes his place with those recent dead of the sib who, like himself, have not achieved deification. As time goes on, he and those like him who have not been translated into the category of family deities manifest their displeasure by harassing their relatives who are alive. As has been seen, this pressure eventually forces the living to carry through the ceremonies which deify the ancestors, the spirit whose journey has been followed thus becoming a full-fledged member of the family pantheon to be summoned back to earth at regular intervals to attend the celebrations of the family dead, and to be called on in time of stress to give his aid.

Though the world of the dead can only be visited in the most unusual circumstances, such visits are believed to have occurred. . . . It will be noted that though reference to ghosts has been made from time to time, the concept of the ghost has thus far not figured in the discussion of the souls of man. Ghosts are called *kudito* ("dead-not-embarked"), which is to say that if the proper funeral ceremonies have not been performed for a man, he wanders between the world of the living and the world of the dead. In order to appease such dissatisfied spirits when they trouble the living, a ceremony called *buyato*—"softening the spirit of the dead"—is performed. Nothing, however, could be learned concerning the nature of this ceremony, nor could further information about the nature of ghosts be obtained. This fact is not without significance, for though the matter was broached in broad daylight, informants would neither discuss ghosts nor this ceremony for "softening them," one saying that those who perform this ceremony and otherwise occupy themselves with ghosts are so powerful that if he talked they would come to his home to ask what right he had to discuss these things.

The question at once arises who these omniscient beings might be. The answer is that they comprise the sorcerers, for in Dahomey, as in so many other Negro cultures, the essence of sorcery lies in obtaining control over a human spirit to do the bidding of the worker of evil magic. Thus it was recounted several times how one individual

125

or another, who was thought to be dead, had been encountered in Togoland or on the Gold Coast or in Nigeria. Such individuals, however, did not recognize their old friends, even though addressed by name. They were soulless beings, whose death was not real but resulted from the machinations of sorcerers who made them appear as dead, and then, when buried, removed them from their graves and sold them into servitude in some far-away land.[1] That ghosts are greatly feared was affirmed by all. An indication of how general that fear is was had when one of the informants who flatly refused to discuss them was found to be a man who was well educated in the European sense of the term, and who by all Dahomean criteria was a skeptic and nonconformist.

One further point in connection with this discussion of the soul must be considered, namely, the extent to which Dahomeans manifest a belief in that classical type of animism which holds that primitives believe in the existence of souls in inanimate objects and animals. It may be asserted that the Dahomean has no such belief. While it is true that animals partake of the *lido*, the "bit of Mawu" which makes living beings of them, yet animals possess no proper *se*. However, the question concerning the nature of the spirits which inhabit the trees and rocks and rivers and mountains held sacred remains to be answered. Here again, the matter is not difficult to explain, says the Dahomean. They cannot be regarded as animated by souls in the sense that human beings are animated. A tree, a rock, a stream which is inhabited by a spirit, possesses only the spirit of a human being. "History tells us of men and women who became angry, and disappeared into trees and rocks. The great Gede rock is regarded as a *vodu*, but that is because long ago the soul of Gede entered it after a quarrel. The water [i.e., lagoon] called Nohwe is a spirit, but that is because the soul of a wife of Adjahuto, whom he told to wash a white cloth red and a red cloth white without giving her any water to do this with, burst from exhaustion and exasperation and became a lake. In the *loko* trees and silk-cotton trees are souls of powerful dead. Not every tree, or rock, or river, however, has a

[1] The correspondence of this belief to that of the *zombi* in Haiti will be obvious to students of Haitian custom.

soul. For those that have—'history has an explanation.'" And though it is true that there are animals who are "respected," just as the Sasa animals described by Rattray among the Ashanti are respected, the reason for this respect and for the ceremonies held over them when killed is not because they have souls, but because of feats performed in the great past which have won for them the right to certain distinctions from the gods or from man.

In an address on "The Significance of West Africa for Negro Research," given at the Twentieth Anniversary of the Association for the Study of Negro Life and History in Chicago on September 10, 1935, Herskovits presented the kinds of evidence used by ethnohistorians in showing that West Africa was the predominant African influence that helped shape the cultures of the Negro peoples of the New World. (See the Introduction to chapter 3 of this book.)

5 The Significance of West Africa for Negro Research *

✤ In two recent papers [1] I have presented a portion of the evidence which, based on the study of historical documents and anthropological field research, indicates the preponderantly West African origin of the Negroes of the New World. In considering the significance of this region for research on the Negro, I may, at the outset, add certain further testimony on this point, gathered by myself in the field, or which has appeared in recent historical publications, not included in these previous discussions of the subject.

* Copyright © 1936 by The Association for the Study of Negro Life and History, Inc. Published in *Journal of Negro History* 21, no. 1 (1936):15–30.
[1] "On the Provenience of New World Negroes," *Journal of Social Forces,* vol. xii (1933), pp. 247–62, and "The Social History of the Negro," in A *Handbook of Social Psychology* (C. Murchison, Editor), Clark University Press, 1935, pp. 207–67.

Melville J. Herskovits

I

One of the most difficult problems for students of the slave trade has been to obtain information concerning the traffic in the interior of the African continent. Current opinion stresses the vast distances which the slave caravans are supposed to have travelled to reach the coastal ports. As has been indicated in the papers cited, this opinion is to be questioned, since not only the available evidence from contemporary sources, but the logic of population distribution and the economics of the trade point toward the forested coastal belt as the locale from which the slaves were principally derived. The assumption of the derivation of slaves from tribes far inland perhaps results from the tendency to measure distance by time. The rate of progress of these caravans was very slow; yet the mere fact that the slave-coffles took a long time to reach the coast from the interior has been held sufficient to justify the assumption that they came from very far countries indeed.

The only definite first-hand statement in the literature that I have been able to discover is the description of the journey of such a caravan given by Mungo Park, who accompanied it in its travels to the sea. This account speaks of five hundred miles as the distance covered in the many weary months the slave-coffle was on its way. Undoubtedly there are other contemporary documents with which I am not familiar; in any event, human documentation concerning the latter days of the slave trade is still possible, and it is this personal testimony, obtained in the city of Kano, in northern Nigeria, in 1931, which is the first portion of the evidence I wish to lay before you today.[2]

Kano has long been an important center in the interior of West Africa. Lying some seven hundred miles from the coast, it was the capital of the Hausa Empire until its absorption into the British Colony of Nigeria, and today retains the economic importance

[2] It is a pleasure to acknowledge the cooperation and aid given me by the Emir of Kano, and by Mr. M. V. Backhouse, then Assistant District Officer in the Nigerian Political Service. Without their help, not only would it have been impossible to obtain the information given here, but I would not even have known of its existence.

which its strategic position as a terminus of numerous Saharan caravan routes gives it. Not so well known is the fact that it is also the terminus of an important trading route toward the southwest, connecting Kano with the territory of the Ashanti and the other peoples of the Gold Coast. And it is this trade that was carried on between Kano and the Gold Coast in human and other merchandise, with which we are concerned.

The data to be given here were obtained from four old men with whom I sat for some hours discussing the details of the trade. The oldest, a man probably well into his nineties, had made his last trip about 1880, when the slave trade was in its final stages, and, of course, had been nearly suppressed as far as supplying the New World was concerned. Yet the lateness of the date should not cause us to under-estimate the importance of this evidence, for it was plain in speaking with these men that the manner in which they carried on operations was the same as that in which their forebears, traders like themselves, had also carried on theirs. The Kano slave dealers constituted an in-formal guild. They consulted together as occasion arose; helped one another in achieving their plans, and accepted the advice and direc-tion of a headman. And this point, which is of significance for our argument, may be stressed at the outset; the merchants with whom I talked neither regarded themselves, nor wished to be regarded, pri-marily as slavers. They were merchants, who, more or less incidental to their general commerce, had slaves in their caravans as carriers and servants and drivers. If the market in the Gold Coast was good or the slaves were bad, they were sold, but it was stressed that the major portion of the slaves in the caravans were brought back to Kano, act-ing in the same capacities they had filled on the way to the coast.

Slaves were obtained through war, by means of raids, because of failure to pay debts, and as a result of gambling, since, under the ex-citement of play, men would often stake themselves when everything else had been lost. Warrior slaves were not so much liked, since often such a person had to be killed for refusing to work, or would run away when the opportunity offered and hence would have to be watched especially closely; while, of course, such men were always the centers of potential trouble. Therefore, the slaves that were taken in war or after a raid were women and children, the men being usually killed in the fighting. Often the pagan peoples among whom the raids were carried out—for the people of Kano are devout Mohammedans—attempted to destroy themselves when it was seen that resistance was useless. The brains of the children would be dashed out, wives would be killed, and, setting fire to their homes, the men would commit suicide. In some cases, a village would be captured by surprise, and the people would be allowed to remain in their homes on condition they pay tribute. This was true of the Bauchi people near Zaria, I was informed, and in such cases the tribute was given in slaves. Thus it seems likely that in a number of instances there were what might be regarded as breeding centers from which slaves were drawn.

When a sufficient number of slaves was on hand, and the amount of merchandise to be sold warranted it, a caravan, normally comprising from one thousand to two thousand persons, would be formed. The journey to the Gold Coast, a distance of some eleven hundred miles by the route taken, plus the return trip, would require two or three years. Of the personnel of a caravan of two thousand, some fourteen hundred would be slaves, the balance being traders, their wives, and their children. The reason, not difficult to see, why a large group of traders would band together in this manner concerned their safety on the march. Tribute was demanded by certain local potentates for the right to pass their countries, and this tribute would be given in kola nuts, which are much relished and not easy to get in this part of Africa, since they grow in the southern forested belt and must be imported. Raids were often attempted by the peoples through whose territory the caravan passed, and, if successful, the traders were robbed of their slaves. About one in every ten caravans was apparently thus raided, which means that about once every two years disaster came to some trading enterprise, since about five groups left Kano annually.

The principal commodities carried by the slaves were morocco leather—which, I may remark, is really Kano leather, since it has its name because it was traded into Europe from Morocco, where it was taken across the desert in camel caravans—native cloths, and a native

130

salt called *natron*. Horses accompanied the caravan, but these were traded for more slaves as soon as the trade route turned to the northwest. Once the journey had begun, the slaves were not confined unless information was obtained from some "good" slave to the effect that a certain one might attempt to escape. If the slaves included a refractory group of men, they might be chained neck to neck even during the daytime, but this was unusual, and only done when their behavior was deemed to warrant such treatment or suspicion had been aroused concerning these men. Occasionally a slave died on the way; some of the casualties were the result of disease, but some of the deaths were due to exhaustion caused by the weight of merchandise each slave was compelled to carry. Yet the deaths were surprisingly small; my informants estimated that a loss of between fifty and seventy out of every thousand slaves in a caravan would be generous.

The two routes taken to the Gold Coast were given in great detail, and later independently checked on the map, where all the points mentioned were found. The most favored way was the northerly one which, after leaving Kano, passed through Sokoto and Dodo to Kwala, where it turned southwest to Wagadugu. From here it proceeded southeast to Tenkodogo, and then ran in a line almost due south from Tamale and Mampong to Kumasi, the capital of the Ashanti Kingdom. The other route began in a direction directly westward from Kano, passing through Djega, where it turned southwest to Ilo and crossed the Niger. Continuing in the same direction through Yendi and Salaga to Mampong, it joined the other route to Kumasi. When asked whether or not trading was carried on to the south into the territory of the Yoruba peoples of Southern Nigeria, or into Dahomey, the reply was negative—for both countries it was said that "the donkey doesn't go there." One great advantage of the routes actually taken was the fact that they lay almost entirely within Hausa territory, or at least in territory where nominal protection of the Hausa Empire was to be had. With the Ashanti, Kano always apparently had close relations, and Ashanti friends told me that the two peoples consider themselves related. Today Ashanti weaving is prominently displayed in the Kano market, while every Ashanti town has its "zongo," where people from the north live their lives according to their own customs, or where Hausa Mohammedan traders can stay as they pass through.

Once in the Gold Coast, slaves and merchandise were disposed of as opportunity offered, and other wares to be taken back and sold in Kano were bought. In the time of the men with whom I talked, a good male slave brought 250,000 cauries (about $25.00), a girl of twelve to thirteen years of age twice that amount, while a boy of like age was worth some 400,000 cauries, or $40.00. Incidentally, it was felt that the blacker the slave the more valuable he was, the reason given being that the darker skinned persons could better stand the sun. Therefore the reddish-colored Fulani were not prized; in addition, they were said to be more difficult to manage on the march and while in captivity. What happened to a slave after he was sold was no affair of the Hausa traders; however, it was remarked that should a slave be retained by his Ashanti master and have children, these children could not be disposed of but remained as "slaves of the land" or serfs of the descendants of their original owners.[3]

Slaves were not sold at regular markets, but wherever anyone would buy them. Often a caravan would be stopped by someone who saw a slave he fancied, and the transaction was concluded then and there. The Hausa, apparently, never sold directly to European dealers, but to the Gold Coast natives, who liked these northern slaves for themselves, employing them as workers in their fields. There were, however, Gold Coast dealers who would go through the country and buy up slaves from their local owners, and these were really middle-men working for white slavers. Slaves, according to the Kano tradition, had then to be got on board ship secretly so as to avoid the native authorities, who did not permit slaves to be exported because they felt this lessened the manpower of the country. But if the regime in the Gold Coast approached that of Dahomey, as I suspect it did, the actual reason was probably that the lucrative nature of the slave trade made it

---

[3] This would seem to be a general West African custom, since exactly the same status was accorded the descendants of slaves in Dahomey, and, indeed, persists today despite French rule, these serfs giving a half of each day's work to the descendants of their masters.

desirable that it be concentrated in the hands of the monarch and his subordinates, and hence private dealing in slaves was discouraged. These Hausa merchants knew also that slaves were taken to Sierra Leone and across the water to the West Indies, of which they had vaguely heard. Only one of them had actually got to the coast. He had never seen a steam vessel, but spoke of slaves exported "in wooden ships, driven by large sacks, which the wind pushed."

This, then, is the account of the interior slave trading as given by men who themselves, and whose ancestors before them, had actually engaged in it. Let us assess these data in the light of our problem. The first point to be considered in this account of the operations of these Kano merchants who, among other wares, dealt in human goods, has to do with the number of slaves that could have reached the coast through their hands. In their discussion of the trade we see that though perhaps six or seven thousand slaves left Kano every year for the Gold Coast, perhaps two-thirds or three-fourths of that number returned north as carriers, the capacity in which they had acted during the southward journey. And though we may suppose that more than five caravans departed from Kano each year when the slave trade was at its height, and that a smaller proportion of slaves than that named were returned as carriers of merchandise, even then the number who arrived at the coastal factories could constitute but a fraction of the enormous numbers of slaves who the records tell us were shipped from Gold Coast ports. Another item, in the account, is the comment on the worth of darker and lighter individuals. If the reddish Fulani were less desirable merchandise, then it would follow that the darker peoples, who live to the south of Kano, would be the ones particularly marked out for raiding rather than these lighter ones to the north.[4]

This information concerning the slave trade represents only a frac-

---

[4] A point of some importance as indicating the reason why the Hausa did so much raiding for slaves when such a relatively small number were taken to the Gold Coast involes the returns accruing to the Kano dealers from the slave trade to the north. Just as leather and other commodities were carried across the Sahara desert to Tunis, Algiers, Morocco and Egypt, so was human merchandise; and it was stated by my informants that the bulk of the slaves exported from Kano went in this direction, rather than toward the coast of the Atlantic Ocean for eventual shipment to the New World.

Melville J. Herskovits

tion of the data that can be obtained on this point in West Africa today, as is indicated in part, for example, by the vivid and touching traditions held by the peoples of the coastal belt, which have already been presented in a previous publication.[5]

II

The hypothesis that the locale of the slave trade was the more restricted region of West Africa, rather than the continent as a whole, and of this region the coastal forested belt rather than the deeper interior, is substantiated then by data of the kind given in the preceding discussion. Furthermore, the study of the customs of such New World Negro peoples as the Bush Negroes of Dutch Guiana, the Jamaicans, the Haitians, the Brazilian and Cuban groups [6]—the only ones who have been studied with any degree of thoroughness— shows that many of their place-names, religious rites, names of deities, and customs of a social and political nature must be referred to tribes living between Cape Three Points and the mouth of the Niger River. The inference again that this is where those slaves lived who most often succeeded in impressing their peculiar customs on the New World Negroes would seem inescapable. Why the considerable numbers of Negroes brought to this hemisphere from the northerly region of the Gambia, and from Loango and the mouth of the Congo, to the south, should have left no more traces of their customs in New World Negro cultures than they did is a difficult question, which we will consider shortly. Whatever the reason, whenever recognizable tribal customs are found in the New World—not generalized West African ones, but those which can be very specifically assigned to a given people or locality—the tribes almost invariably represented are those of the Gold Coast, Dahomey, and eastern and western Nigeria.

It will perhaps have been remarked that in all the preceding dis-

[5] M. J. and F. S. Herskovits, "A Footnote to the History of Negro Slaving," *Opportunity* 11 (1933): 178–81.
[6] Numerous references to the literature on these cultures will be found in the papers cited at the beginning of this article.

cussion, the emphasis has been on New World rather than American Negroes. This, of course, assumes that the types found in this country are the same as those of the West Indies, of the Guianas, and of Brazil. And, since all evidence tends to show that there was a great deal of commerce in slaves between the various parts of the New World (Brazil excepted), this assumption may be regarded as a truism concerning which it is not necessary to give further testimony.[7] But we must realize that in speaking of the origins of New World Negroes, we are presumably, at least, speaking of the origins of American Negroes. And, conversely, if documentary material can be obtained to show the sources from which the ships that came to the ports of the United States obtained their cargoes, this will throw further light on the question which is under analysis here by indicating the origins of New World Negroes in general.

Let us, therefore, turn to this other type of evidence. To make my point I shall draw on the magnificent body of material which the research of Professor Elizabeth Donnan, aided by the Carnegie Institution of Washington, has recently made available to us. . . .[8]

In [her] last volume [4] Miss Donnan devotes many pages to tables summarizing the manifests of ships arriving at the ports of Maryland, Virginia, South Carolina, and Georgia. Here one finds, among other data, the numbers of slaves carried by each vessel, and the ports from which this human cargo had been obtained. The materials for Maryland and Georgia are fragmentary, but those for Virginia and especially for South Carolina are extremely full, and I have therefore tabulated these data in calculating totals for the various areas from which the slaves were derived. . . .

We may now consider the derivation of slaves imported into South Carolina, as given by Miss Donnan: [9]

[7] See, however, the table cited below for some figures on Negroes imported into the South from West Indian ports.
[8] Elizabeth Donnan, "Documents Illustrative of the History of the Slave Trade to America," Carnegie Institution Publication No. 409 (Washington: The Carnegie Institution of America, 1930–1935), 1:x, 495; 2:xii, 731; 3:xiii, 477; 4:xv, 719.
[9] Donnan, "History of the Slave Trade," 4:310, *passim*.

Melville J. Herskovits

SLAVES IMPORTED INTO SOUTH CAROLINA, 1752–1808 [10]

Source of origin given as "Africa"	4,146
From the Gambia to Sierra Leone	12,441 .
Sierra Leone	3,906
Liberia and the Ivory Coast (i.e., Rice and Grain Coasts)	3,851
"Guinea Coast" (Gold Coast to Calabar)	18,240
Angola	11,485
Congo	10,924
Mozambique	243
East Africa	230
	———
Slaves brought direct from Africa	65,466
Slaves imported from the West Indies	2,303
	———
TOTAL	67,769

It can be seen from the above tabulation how . . . these data corroborate the evidence gathered in comparative studies of the customs of New World Negro groups and West African peoples. For instance, one can understand why it is not surprising that the drum to be seen in the British Museum, collected from the Negroes of Virginia during the latter portion of the eighteenth century, should be similar even in detail to those used today by the Ashanti and Fanti of the Gold Coast. Furthermore, the figures given for the number of Negroes brought either from or via the West Indian Islands (there is not sufficient time or space to detail this in the tables as presented here, but in many instances such designations as "Gold Coast and Jamaica," or "Jamaica [Gambia]" are indicated), also tend to point the assumption that the stocks represented in the United States are no different than those found in the islands. . . .[11]

Let us now consider further the failure to find in the New World Negro culture where Africanisms are to be discovered, such as those

[10] Where, in the tables of Miss Donnan's book, two African sources are given for a cargo of slaves, the number in the cargo has been divided equally between the two regions for the purposes of computation.
[11] In the tables in Miss Donnan's "Documents" giving the sources of slaves imported into the ports of New York and New Jersey during the years 1715–1765 (3:462–512), of a total of 4,457, only 930, or 21 percent, came directly from Africa.

136

of the Guianas, or Haiti, or Jamaica, more than the slightest trace of either Senegalese or Congo traditions. The most likely explanation is that the peoples strongly represented in the days of the height of the slave traffic established their own tribal customs so that those in the minority, or those who came later, would have to adapt themselves to the patterns of behavior they found in vogue. Miss Donnan's tables indicate this in the case of the Congo Negroes, for in the lists of South Carolina importations of slaves, except for a few very early cargoes, by far the greater number of Congo Negroes figure in manifests dating toward the end of the trade, after the Guinea Coast was patrolled by the warships of Britain and France, while the numbers of Angola importations likewise increase materially in the later lists.

III

I have presented the material contained in this paper to point the fact of the great significance of West Africa for Negro research. If it is true, as I think must be apparent from the evidence which other workers in the field of Negro studies have discovered, and other data such as those which I have placed before you today, that New World Negroes are descended mainly from West African stocks, then the paramount importance of having adequate knowledge of the physical types, the customs, and beliefs, and the languages of the peoples of this region, is not difficult to see. It is not necessary to detail here the many questions which are raised whose answers may perhaps be obtained from an attack that emphasizes, on the African side, this forested belt of the West Coast as the principal locale for study. Thus, the problem of racial crossing is not only of paramount scientific importance, but of practical concern as well. Yet to study Negro-White crossing we must have much more knowledge of the physical types of West Africa than the fragmentary information that is now available. Or, there is the matter of the origins of American Negro speech, or the music of New World Negroes that has been so eagerly debated. Most statements on these points are obviously *ex cathedra*. Though the persons who have analyzed these phenomena have been familiar with European speech or music, they have obviously not been acquainted with the African material that is richly available, either at first-hand or through the literature. In the matter of speech, it is hoped that future research, which will include intensive work in the many grammars and dictionaries of African tongues, will help resolve the question; at the present time, the analysis and transcription by Dr. M. Kolinski, an expert in the study of primitive music, of songs recorded by myself in various field-trips to Dutch Guiana, West Africa, and Haiti, already shows results which assure us that their publication will alter profoundly our theories of the derivation of the spirituals.

Similar questions are posed in the field of culture. The traditions of African origin peculiar to New World Negroes persist in those portions of the United States even where the strongest acculturation to European patterns of behavior has taken place. Equipped with an understanding of African and West Indian Negro cultures, the resemblances are not at all difficult to discern.[12] They invade all fields of Negro life, and, as I have recently had occasion to observe, have invaded the life of white Americans—to say nothing of white West Indians—as well.[13] And the practical importance of recognizing the complex and advanced character of the West African civilizations from which New World Negroes came, and thus removing the unfortunate and undeserved stigma of the "savage" character of the African which, I regret to say, exists as strongly in the thinking of American Negroes as it does in the minds of American Whites, should be patent.

One final question may be asked. Is not this insistence on concentrated study of West Africa one of those obvious points with which everyone agrees? Why should the point be argued at all? The answer lies in the fact that American students of the Negro have, with a few noteworthy exceptions, almost utterly failed to do more than lip service to the necessity for West African study. To go to West Africa is costly, and, from certain points of view, dangerous. But it is no less costly, though somewhat less dangerous, to go to

---

[12] The extent to which there has been a reluctance to admit, or inability to discern, the African character of many of these traditions and modes of behavior is not without psychological interest as indicating how deep-seated patterns of thought can invade scientific research.

[13] "What Has Africa Given America?", *The New Republic* 84 (1935):92–94.

South Africa, or East Africa, or North Africa, as American students of the scientific problems of the Negro have done and are doing at this moment. I do not wish to decry the importance of study in these other regions. But it seems that with the knowledge that we have of the West African derivation of the American Negroes, and of their affiliation with the Negroes of the New World in general, studies in the scientific problems of the Negro made by those coming from this side of the Atlantic should be concentrated, for purposes of scientific strategy, on the peoples of West Africa. We know relatively little of their manner of living; we know even less of their history. This material is to be had for the seeking, and, when we have it, and compare it with the data to be gained from more intensive scientific study of the Negroes in America and the rest of the New World than has heretofore been undertaken, facts will be at hand not only of inestimable value in giving basic information to those concerned with the practical problems of race relations, but also for the study of one of the most important scientific problems known at the present time —the study of the processes and results of cultural and physical contacts between peoples of different races and differing traditions. In the final analysis, experience has taught us that in matters requiring scientific study, the longest way around is most often the shortest route to a given point. And it is thus likely that more preoccupation with the background of Negro life, and fewer conclusions drawn from insufficient knowledge of fundamentals may be the way to achieve happier results in the practical problems of race and racial relations with which we are all, as citizens, concerned.

Perhaps the best brief statement of Herskovits' conception of the field of Afroamerican Studies is found in the paper he read at the sessions of the Primer Congreso Demográfico Interamericano *sponsored by the* Instituto Internacional de Estudios Afroamericanos *in the Castillo de Chapultepec, Mexico City, on October 20,*

1943. In this paper, titled "Problem, Method and Theory in Afro-american Studies," Herskovits asserted that "Afroamerican studies not only cross disciplines, but are inter-continental, treating of peoples living in North, South and Central America, the Caribbean, and Africa. . . . Here can be prosecuted those comparative researches of mixtures of physical type, of languages and of modes of behavior in terms of known rather than of assumed past contact. . . ."

6 Problem, Method and Theory in Afroamerican Studies *

I

✛ This paper will discuss three elements in the scientific study of the New World Negro and his African background that, hitherto in large measure implicit in my writings on the subject, suggest their timeliness for explicit formulation. These comprise a definition and delimitation of the field, which is essential for clarity of purpose in research and for directing future effort; some of the methodological concepts and techniques that have been successfully employed; and some of the hypotheses which have guided investigation and developed out of experience in the field.

It is not always realized how recent is systematic study of the Afro-american field. Little of the present substantial store of facts concerning New World cultures, or the civilizations from which they derive, or the historical circumstances of their formation were available two decades ago, so that it is apparent why the need to amass data took first place in the attention of students. This continuing emphasis was particularly relevant in view of the vastness of the area in which New World Negroes live and the variety of their cultures, the complexity of the African civilizations from which they derive, the technical difficulties in the way of studying provenience and the intricacy of the acculturative processes to which they have been exposed.

Today, the scientific importance of Afroamerican studies as a field for research is firmly established. A climate of opinion, both lay and

* Reprinted from Afroamerica 1 (1945):5–24.

scholarly, which encourages further research, has been created, while the body of factual materials and comparative analyses that has been amassed by those working in the field allows hypotheses and procedures to be assessed in terms of collected data and achieved results rather than of probable validity and possible return. It thus appears a logical moment for stock-taking, for the explicit statement of theoretical assumptions, and for a refinement of techniques.

II

An outstanding characteristic of the field of Afroamerican studies is its interdisciplinary nature, which must be taken into account whenever problems of definition or method are under discussion. But more than that, Afroamerican studies not only cross disciplines, but are also inter-continental, treating of peoples living in North, South, and Central America, the Caribbean, and Africa. The implications of this interdisciplinary and intercontinental scope, when thought of in terms of the conventional organization of scholarly study, are many. For the field cuts across so many boundaries that it cannot be defined in terms of any commonly accepted categories—a fact that accounts for its late recognition as a definable area of scholarship and for certain practical difficulties that at one time or another have faced those who have worked on its many problems.

That the ramifications of such studies extend into the social sciences, the humanities, and the biological sciences follows from the nature of the data. In this our field is no different from any research that is concerned with obtaining a rounded view of the life of man, or of any group of men. It is nonetheless worthwhile to recall how in Afroamerican studies investigation has had to have recourse to the resources of anthropology, history, and psychology to reach an understanding of the social structures, the accepted patterns of behavior, and the past development of the societies studied; how linguistics, musicology, and comparative literature have had to be called upon to contribute their techniques for insight into some of the most revealing data in the field; and how such problems as the incidence and effects of race-crossing, of the dynamics of Negro population formation, and the like have had to be studied in terms of the techniques and orienta-

141

tions of human biology and demography. Not every student can study every problem, but most students of the Negro have come to realize that their competence in the discipline of their primary affiliation gives them but a starting-point for further effort; and that their field of interest has characteristically broadened as the data have been followed where they led, even when these called for disregard of current delimitation of scholarly concern.

In similar fashion, accepted regional approaches to the ordering of research have had to be transcended. Researches restricted to Latin American problems, or to the United States, or to Africa or to an island of the Caribbean alone, of course, make their contributions to Afroamerican studies. For where data are as sparse as in this field, all contributions are welcome. But those whose perspectives have not been so circumscribed know well how much researches in these areas are enriched by a broader point of view. One of the most telling instances of this is the aid which the study of New World Negro peoples can bring toward a fuller comprehension of the cultures of Africa itself. This is striking because it reverses the customary order of thought, which focuses on African survivals in the New World. That the study of African ways of life is essential to an understanding of survivals of these customs is a truism; but what, it may be asked, can the analysis of survivals contribute to comprehension of their own sources?

Though the matter cannot be documented here, it need merely be recalled that survival is an index of tenacity, which in turn reveals general orientations in parent cultures that may at times not be given proper stress without such background. This is the case as concerns the place of religion in African cultures, whose theoretical importance will be considered in a later page. Furthermore, specific complexes of significance that have been quite overlooked in Africanist studies are to be revealed by investigation on this side of the Atlantic. A recent example of this is had in the instance of the place of drummers, not only in cult-rituals, but in the life of the community as a whole. First noted in a New World Negro culture, it required only brief questioning of Africans to reveal itself as an important facet of social organization in Africa itself, that had hitherto not been explored at all. [See section on Ethnohistory in chapter 8.]

Though overlapping many disciplines and a number of geographical regions, the field of Afroamerican studies is distinct from all those on which it impinges, from which it follows that it is therefore often a matter of emphasis and intent just where a given piece of research is to be classified. This is the source of many practical difficulties. Papers on African cultures, deriving from studies stimulated by an interest in the New World descendants of Africa, may appear in Africanist journals where much of their usefulness to those who concentrate on New World Negro societies is lost, while reports on historical aspects of the field, often published in historical journals, are not seen by those studying Afroamerican problems whose primary affiliation is with other disciplines. Conversely Africanists who confine their work to the peoples of that continent, or historians of the Negro whose range of interest is defined by their discipline, fail to benefit from New World studies, or from work on other than historical phases of Negro life that might open new vistas to them.

This may meet with the reasonable suggestion that there is enough justification for the existence of the conventional disciplines in their achieved results to give us pause before we cross their boundaries, tested by time and experience. In the final analysis, however, the ordering of the most fruitful results can be had only when the facts are studied as they lie, without those preconceptions which, in a case such as that under discussion, lead to distortion if not considered in terms of all interrelated aspects.

This leads us to the nature of the contributions Afroamerican studies can be expected to make, for the point is basic in discussing the importance of the field for scientific research. More than anything else, it comprises data that, because of the available historic controls and the range of related materials, go far toward approximating those laboratory situations which, in the study of man, are more difficult to achieve than any other single methodological factor in the repertory of science. Thus the very fact that to conduct Afroamerican studies calls on the techniques of many disciplines, and is carried on in many different areas, gives it a special significance for the scientific study of man. For here can be prosecuted those comparative researches of mixtures of physical types, of languages, and of modes of behavior in terms of known rather than of assumed past contacts. And while in this Afroamerican research does not differ in kind from studies among other groups of differing backgrounds between whom contact has taken place or is in process, it is to be distinguished from them in degree, as expressed in the very broad variety of situations that, in this field, are to be investigated.

It is not difficult to phrase the manner in which the Afroamerican field differs from the several disciplines on which it draws. To the extent that its problems are to be comprehended within their areas of interest, such problems have an affiliation immediately recognizable. Thus a study of land-tenure in a Caribbean island might find ready reception in a journal devoted to economics, the analysis of a Negro musical style in a musicological publication, the description of the physical characteristics of a North American Negro community in an organ devoted to the problems of physical anthropology. Even where cross-disciplinary considerations have entered, publication can be achieved in journals devoted to the discipline of principal emphasis or, more often, in the subject with which the student is technically affiliated. This is one of the reasons why bibliographic problems are so difficult in Afroamerican research.

To draw the line between area fields and Afroamerican research requires somewhat more careful distinctions, for here the problem of efficient historic relationships enters. It is simple to state that study of the Negro in Latin America contributes to the Latin American field; even though, in this sense, we once again encounter overlapping. Yet it is open to question how much a detailed investigation of certain Negro social conventions or music or religious beliefs that have not significantly diffused to other population elements in a given Latin American country is to be regarded as a contribution to the Latin American field, except in a secondary sense.

In the Africanist field, the matter is somewhat different. In earlier years, before the provenience of New World Negroes was known as well as it is at present, it was held that a knowledge of African culture in general was essential to effective comparative study of the New World Negro. Today, however, one may ask why, except for general background, this is needed. Field research on the cultures of East Africa, the study of the slave trade in Zanzibar, the analysis of Bushman art, or investigation of Zulu physical types deal with peoples who are outside the range of effective historic impact on New World Negro patterns, since so few individuals from the parts of Africa where they live were brought to the New World that their influence in the formation of New World Negro types and cultures could only have been negligible.

A further point to be made in clarifying the limits of the Afroamerican field has to do with the study of those situations of everyday life in many countries which, as they affect the Negro, present practical problems of great moment that press for immediate solutions. Because the student is also the citizen, with heightened awareness of the needs engendered by these situations, the temptation is great to give over the long-term view in favor of *ad hoc* solutions of such issues. This has been especially true in the United States, where for many years an almost exclusive preoccupation with action programs discouraged the type of broad research which characterizes the Afroamerican field. This is not the place to consider the problem of applied science as against research on a long-term basis, yet it is important that the distinction be made and maintained. For even in the short view, the broader base of comprehension that the results of Afroamerican studies can give those whose task is to frame policies for practical procedures would, of itself, justify the position that such studies must be held distinct from remedial programs in the troubled field of race relations.

Finally, it must be stressed that Afroamerican studies are not to be limited to the study of Negro populations and their cultures alone, but must follow through to assess the contributions Africa has made to the peoples among whom the Negroes live. Thus when race-crossing carries Negroid elements into the genetic composition of the non-Negroid groups, this is quite as significant a subject for research as it is to determine the physical traits of the Negroid group. Parallel cultural phenomena have not been systematically studied at all, except, perhaps, in Brazil. Yet just as race-crossing invariably follows on contact between peoples of different physical types, so cultural borrowing —two-way borrowing—also ensues. The theoretical importance of this fact is clear. Here the problem is stated to emphasize the necessity of including, in the repertory of Afroamerican research, investigation not only into the maintenance of African tradition in the New World, but also into how, and to what extent African custom was diffused to the aboriginal Indian peoples and to those of European derivation who experienced prolonged contact with Africans and their descendants.

III

To the extent that the problems of Afroamerican research fall within the compass of established disciplines, or require interdisciplinary consideration of a type already employed outside the Afroamerican field, the question of method presents no difficulty. A comparative study of Negro music utilizes the techniques of the musicologist, one of language employs the methods of the linguists, research into the present-day Negro family or of living standards of Negro populations uses the approaches of the sociologist or the economist. Overall descriptions of any of these cultures, whether in Africa or the New World, require ethnological field techniques, while analyses of psychological problems arising out of the way of life of Negro peoples utilizes the methods of social psychology. Studies of the slave trade, or of the economics of the plantation, though cross-disciplinary, find research techniques at hand in the modes of investigation employed by economic historians.

Strangely enough, the resources of ethnology and history have only recently been welded into a usable tool. Despite the fact that there are historical schools of ethnology and social historians, there has been but little contact across these disciplines. The "history" of these ethnological schools has been based on the reconstruction of events rather than on documentation; while the social historian, despite the illumination his writings have thrown on the development of the institutions with which he has dealt, has worked primarily as an historian and only rarely and recently has had recourse to the methods of the social sciences. There are, of course, some exceptions to this statement. Studies of certain Indian groups in the United States afford instances of how the use of historic sources has been able to illuminate ethnographic problems, while historians of the American frontier are more and more finding it essential to take into account the relevant ethnographic facts.

Experience is teaching us that the methods of these two disciplines, more than any other two, must be jointly called on if the varying situations that are to be studied comparatively in the Afroamerican field are to be analyzed with comprehension. It must be stressed that this field, constituting as it does a special instance of culture contact, derives its greatest significance from the fact that it so superbly documents the problems of cultural dynamics. Now in studies of culture contact it is essential to establish the cultural base-lines from which the processes of change began, to know facts concerning the culture or cultures that have emerged, or are emerging from the contact, and to comprehend how, and under what circumstances, the phenomena as observed in the culture that has resulted from the contact actually developed. The first of these requires ethnographic study, and in some measure the second. But the second also requires historical treatment, while the third demands an attack that is essentially historical.

The *ethnohistorical method*, as this combined ethnological and historical approach is to be termed, has been basic in systematic Afroamerican research, for until the use of this method was fully established, it was found difficult to achieve perspective, and comparative studies were but elusive. It is through the use of this method, and only by its use, that it has been possible to recover the predominant regional and tribal origins of the New World Negroes and, with this information in hand, to turn to ethnographic research in Africa with a certainty that the materials gathered there would be relevant to the problems of cultural retention and cultural change encountered in the New World. Similarly this method makes it possible to test the validity of the rich store of existing documentary information concerning slaves and slaving, plantation life and the responses of the Negro to it, and the like, and to realize much of the potential contribution of these materials. Most important, also, has been the continuous comparison of ethnographic facts as found on the two sides of the Atlantic; for ethnohistory, as employed in the study of Afroamerican problems, consists essentially of the application of a comparative ethnographic technique in unravelling, on the basis of written sources, the historic progression of events that led up to the establishment and functioning of New World Negro cultures as they exist at the present time.

Not only has the ethnohistorical approach been able to fix the African origins of New World Negro cultures, but it has been of great value in accounting for differences that are found between the cultures of Negroes living in different parts of the New World. Thus comparative ethnographic studies have revealed that the cultures of the Dutch Guiana Bush Negroes and of the Maroons of Jamaica manifest their Africanisms predominantly in terms of Gold Coast retentions, while those of Haiti are of Dahomean and Yoruba derivation. The documents tell us that Dutch and English planters preferred Gold Coast slaves, not only because they were more likely to find these for sale by their own nationals, but because of rationalizations that came to be set up concerning the worth of Negroes from tribes of this area compared to other kinds of Negroes. On the other hand, they make it equally clear that Latin slave owners preferred Dahomean and Yoruba slaves, for the same reasons, and thus resolve what would otherwise be a difficult problem.

Another methodological device that has proved of outstanding value in analyzing the problems of Afroamerican research is that of a scale of intensity of Africanisms over the New World. This implies a logically conceived continuum which ranges from retentions that are completely African, or almost so, to those least African and most European—the Indian elements having been so little studied that they cannot be classified. Such a continuum permits an arrangement of the data that gives insight into the processes of cultural change by allowing comparisons to be drawn between cultures whose various aspects lie at different points on it. This, in turn, facilitates analysis of the processes that have operated to bring about the cultural changes observed in the course of field research.

It must be emphasized that, as in all scientific study, a classificatory device such as the scale of intensity of Africanisms is but a means to an end rather than an end in itself. In this case, the end that is envisaged is that comprehension of process which alone can lead to valid prediction. To be revealing in terms of this end the classification must be derived through induction, and flow from the data, rather than be imposed upon it after the fashion of *a priori* categories that tend to force materials into groupings that do violence to the scientific reality. Scientific analysis is impossible without classification of data, and herein lies the importance of this series of categories; but it cannot be too strongly emphasized that classification, of itself, can tell us nothing about causes, or relationships, or the processes of change.

A *scale of intensity of Africanisms* was first established somewhat more than a decade ago. At that time, however, the data were meager compared with present resources, so that of necessity the listing was tentative, and had to be in terms of whole cultures or areas or countries. That is, places were assigned to such Negro groups as those of the Guianas or the Virgin Islands, or Haiti, on a scale ranging from most to least African. A revision of this original statement was made several years later, but still in overall terms, though additional data from various regions were utilized to amplify and rectify the listing. While preferable to the earlier statement, this revision proved to be simpler than the nature of the materials has come to demand. For overall categories of this character do not adequately illuminate the complexities of the data, and often indeed hide relationships rather than reveal them, which is their intent.

The scale given in this paper represents an application to Afro-american studies of certain techniques of analyzing cultures that have been increasingly employed as greater acquaintance with human ways of living has been gained. That is, we now know that the broad divisions of culture, even particular institutions, behave differently in different situations. This does not mean that a given body of tradition is to be thought of as other than a unified whole, whose elements are all closely interrelated. But it has come to be recognized that the historic forces that are operative in any given situation— forces which, by their very nature, are unique in each circumstance—

will eventuate differently in different instances as far as differing aspects of culture are concerned, or where different institutions within a given cultural category are involved.

The principle of cultural focus, discussed in later pages, is helpful in this connection, since its implications for the dynamics of culture in this situation, as in all others, is that it offers an important leverage to bring about changes in certain aspects of a people's way of life as against others or, under contact, to make for differential resistance to change. Thus pressures from outside the Negro groups to give over economic patterns were far greater in the New World than those militating against the retention of folktales or secular musical forms, so that the latter two manifest far more of an African character than the former. On the other hand, inner compulsions derived from the focal concerns of Africans with the supernatural tended to resist varying pressures, in varying countries, employing the different kinds of adjustments that have been described, with the result that Africanisms figure prominently in New World Negro religious behavior everywhere.

A refinement of the earlier scale of intensity of Africanisms, not in terms of total cultures, but of aspects within each culture, such as our data now make possible, is given here. In addition, a further refinement has been achieved by subdividing the areas which earlier appeared as units, where the materials indicate that within a given region districts can be distinguished wherein the pattern and degree of African retentions differ. But since it is apparent that in every part of the New World where Negroes live, excepting only the Guiana Bush, class differences operate so as to make for variation in the number and intensity of Africanisms within each Negro group, our table will record only that degree of retention for each group which is closest to African custom.

Because this point is crucial for a proper reading of the table, and an adequate understanding of its significance, it may be amplified here. Bahia, for example, is rated as most African in language because only there have certain African tongues been retained, as against retention, at most, of no more than African words or phrases or grammatical structures elsewhere. In their daily usage, as a matter of fact, the Bahian Negroes show perhaps less African elements than elsewhere, since they speak the same Portuguese as is spoken by other Brazilians, with fewer elements of African vocabulary, pronunciation, or grammar than is found in the speech of almost any other New World Negro group.

It cannot be too strongly stressed that in every area of the New World, except in the Guiana Bush, variation in African forms of behavior stretches from the point of greatest intensity indicated in our table to almost conformity with European ways of life. The problem thus becomes one of accounting for differing degrees of variability in the different populations studied. But since the variation in almost every case does extend to the limit set by the conventions of European custom, it can be seen how significant is the analysis of retentions of African convention if we are to discover how far the distribution extends toward the patterns that made up the cultural endowment of the ancestors of present day Negro populations that are the central concern of Afroamerican research.

Table 1 presents, then, these degrees of intensities of Africanisms, listed by aspect of culture and by region in terms of the most African-like manifestation of a given cultural aspect or institution. The assignment of values in each instance has either been on the basis of my own field research in the regions listed, or on the reports of trained and competent observers in areas where I have not had first-hand contact. The weightings given the entries are broadly conceived, as is indicated by the terms used to denote the categories of intensity— "very African," "quite African," and the like. To be more specific would be merely to enlarge the area of possible disagreement between students, and to no purpose, since all classifications of such data must be subjective, at least at this point in our knowledge and with the technical resources for cultural analysis at hand. The sources are indicated in the note appended to the text of this paper.

Greater refinement in the treatment of these data might also be more revealing, but the technique of trait-analysis seems to be too mechanical, and to work too great violence to the unity of the cultural elements involved, to be profitably employed in this case. In like manner, the designations are to be regarded as having been set down

TABLE 1 *

SCALE OF INTENSITY OF NEW WORLD AFRICANISMS
(Only the greatest degree of retention is indicated for each group)

	Tech-nology	Eco-nomic	Social Organi-zation	Non-kinship Institutions	Reli-gion	Magic	Art	Folk-lore	Music	Lan-guage
Guiana (bush)	b	b	a	a	a	a	b	a	a	b
Guiana (Paramaribo)	c	c	b	c	a	a	e	a	a	c
Haiti (peasant)	c	b	b	c	a	a	d	a	a	c
Haiti (urban)	e	d	c	c	b	b	e	a	a	c
Brazil (Bahia-Recife)	d	d	b	d	a	a	b	a	a	a
Brazil (Porto Alegre)	e	e	c	d	a	a	e	a	a	c
Brazil (Maranhão-rural)	c	c	b	e	c	b	e	b	b	d
Brazil (Maranhão-urban)	e	d	c	e	a	b	e	d	a	b
Cuba	e	d	c	b	a	a	b	b	a	a
Jamaica (Maroons)	c	c	b	b	b	a	e	a	a	c
Jamaica (Morant Bay)	e	c	b	b	a	a	e	a	a	a
Jamaica (general)	e	c	d	d	b	b	e	a	b	c
Honduras (Black Caribs) **	c	c	b	b	b	a	e	b	c	e
Trinidad (Port of Spain)	e	d	c	b	a	a	e	b	a	e
Trinidad (Toco)	e	d	c	c	c	b	e	b	b	d
Mexico (Guerrero)	d	e	b	b	c	b	e	b	?	e
Columbia (Choco)	d	d	c	c	c	b	e	b	a	e

Virgin Islands	e	d	c	d	e	b	e	b	b	d
U.S. (Gullah Islands)	c	c	c	d	c	b	e	a	b	b
U.S. (rural South)	d	e	c	d	c	b	e	b	b	e
U.S. (urban North)	e	e	c	d	c	b	e	d	b	e

a: very African b: quite African c: somewhat African d: a little African e: trace of African customs, or absent ?: no report

* The derivations of the listings given in Table I are as follows:

Guiana, *Brazil* (Bahia and southern Brazil), *Trinidad*, and *Haiti*, field research, and various published works bearing on the Negro peoples of these countries.

Brazil (north-urban and rural), unpublished reports of fieldwork by Octavio Eduardo in Maranhão.

Jamaica, first-hand contact with the Maroons and other Jamaican Negroes, though without opportunity for detailed field research; and for the general population, the volume *Black Roadways in Jamaica*, by Martha Beckwith.

Cuba, various works by F. Ortiz, particularly his *Los Negros Brujos*, and on R. Lachetáneré's *Manuel de Santeria*.

Virgin Islands, the monograph by A. A. Campbell entitled, "St. Thomas Negroes—a Study of Personality and Culture" (*Psychological Monographs*, 55, no. 5 [1943]), and unpublished field materials of J. C. Trevor.

Gullah Islands, field-work by W. R. Bascom, some results of which have been reported in a paper entitled, "Acculturation among the Gullah 'Negroes'" (*American Anthropologist*, 43, [1941,]:43–50).

United States, many works, from which materials of African derivation have been abstracted and summarized in my own work, *The Myth of the Negro Past*.

** Carib Indian influences are strong in this culture.

Melville J. Herskovits

for convenience only, and to consider them as anything more than useful symbols would be to introduce a note of spurious accuracy against which too great warning cannot be given.

It is apparent, from scanning the table, that the overall listings in the earlier ratings are in the main borne out by the tabulations of this more refined treatment, the principal clarification being in the direction of indicating variability of retention within a given country. Especially interesting is the indication that extension of the continuum toward the pole of African traditions can be greater in certain traits manifested in centers of population than in Brazil. Taken as a whole, however, the progression of Guiana, Haiti, Brazil, Jamaica, Trinidad, Cuba, Virgin Islands, the Gullah Islands, and southern and northern United States comprise a series wherein a decreasing intensity of Africanisms is manifest. The series will be filled in after field-work has been carried on in areas as yet unstudied, but there seems little prospect of finding New World Negro cultures more African than those of the interior of Dutch Guiana, nor, in recognizable form, less so than among certain Negro groups in the northern part of the United States.

Turning now to consider the different degree to which differing elements in each of these cultures have responded to contact with non-African ways of life, we see that the carry-over of Africanisms is anything but uniform over the individual cultures, being far greater in some aspects than in others. Certain generalizations can, however, be drawn. Music, folklore, magic and religion, on the whole, have retained more of their African character than economic life, or technology, or art, while language and social structures based on kinship or free association tend to vary through all the degrees of intensity that are noted.

These differences are probably due to the circumstances of slave life, and confirm common sense observations made during the period of slavery. Slave owners were primarily concerned with the technological and economic aspects of the lives of their slaves, while the conditions of life as a slave also of necessity warped whatever patterns of African social structures the Negroes felt impelled to preserve. On the other hand, what tales were told or the songs that were sung

154

made little difference to the masters, and few external blocks were placed in the way of their retention. In the case of religion, outer controls were of varying kinds and were responded to in varying degree, as is reflected in the intermediate position of this cultural element. Magic, which tends to go underground under pressure and can most easily be practiced without direction—the force of the specific psychological compulsions here being of special importance—persisted in recognizable form everywhere, particularly since the similarity between African and European magic is so great that the one cultural stream must have operated to reinforce the other. The failure of African art to survive except in Guiana and to a lesser degree in Brazil is understandable when the life of the slave, which permitted little leisure and offered slight stimulus for the production of art in the aboriginal African style or, indeed, in any other style, is recalled.

One further fact which emerges from our table is the differing variability, over the New World as a whole, of the several aspects of the cultures as these have been listed. Only religion and language comprehend in maximum extension toward African patterns all degrees of intensity. Minimum variation in this respect is shown by music, which everywhere has been retained in at least "quite African" form. The degree of variation within each of the groups is likewise interesting, since it is seen how the Bush-Negro culture, the most African, is also most homogeneous as far as the African nature of its several elements is concerned, while the cultures of the Negroes of the United States, though manifesting a comparable degree of homogeneity, expresses its homogeneous quality at the opposite end of the scale.

The facts thus shown hold both particular and general significance. To students of Afroamerican problems, differentials offer leads for further historical and ethnological analysis, since it is to be assumed that the explanation for such differentials is to be discovered in the modes of conducting slaving operations and in the circumstances of slave life, as these reacted upon the aboriginal patterns of individuals derived from the various relevant cultures of Africa. From the broader point of view of understanding culture as a whole, however, such treatment documents the concept of culture as a series of interrelated, but quasi-independent variables that undergo processes of change in accordance with the particular historical situation under which impact of new ideas and new customs has taken place, and the focal concerns of the peoples who, like the Negroes of the New World, made the cultural and psychological adjustments that were called forth by their historical experience.

IV

The hypotheses that underlie the study of African cultural survivals in the New World derive from a conception of human civilization that holds social behavior to be something learned rather than inborn and instinctive. This means that though there are as many cultures—that is, accepted modes of conduct, configurations of institutions, and systems of values and goals—as there are societies, every culture, or any of its elements, can be mastered by any individual without regard to race, or by any group that has the will and the opportunity to master it.

It follows from our concept of culture as something learned that the borrowing of traditions by one people from another is a simple matter, and research has actually established that cultural borrowing is a universal in human social experience. It is today clear that no two peoples have ever been in contact but that they have taken new ideas and new customs from each other, and this quite independently of whether that contact was friendly or hostile, whether it was between groups of the same size or of unequal size, whether differences of prestige existed between them or they met on a plane of equality.

The conception of culture on which our hypotheses are based thus envisages the operation of the principle of constant change—through borrowing and internal innovation—but at the same time assumes a high degree of stability in every culture, which is assured by the transmission of habits, customs, beliefs, and institutions from one generation to the next. That is, the individual member of a society learns how to behave in a given situation, how to operate the techniques which assure his society its living, how to adapt to a given system of drives, rewards and values because he is taught or observes all these things. The resultant cultural conservatism gives to every way of life a tenaciousness, a toughness—in many writings not sufficiently recognized—which comes to be of special importance in the study of Africanisms among the Negroes of the New World.

If we assume, then, that culture is in constant change because it is learned, and not inborn, but is learned by the individuals that constitute any given society so well that the tendency of human beings to conserve tradition gives to every culture great stability, the problem next presented is to resolve this seeming paradox by studying those circumstances in which changes are instituted, or in which retention of conventions makes for successful resistance to change. It is essentially the problem of balancing the drives that induce acceptance of new customs as against the mechanisms that preserve earlier sanctioned modes of behavior. It is here that the field of Afroamerican studies can make its greatest contribution.

We may say that the basic hypothesis of culture as something learned is sharpened when it is perceived that under contact elements of a culture are the more effectively retained in the degree that they bear resemblance to newly experienced patterns of behavior or institutions. This, in turn, is further refined by references to the process of *syncretism*, the tendency to identify those elements in the new culture with similar elements in the old one, enabling the persons experiencing the contact to move from one to the other, and back again, with psychological ease. The outstanding instance of syncretism is the identification, in Catholic countries of the New World, of African deities with the saints of the Church—a phenomenon so well documented that it need but be mentioned here to make the point. [See section on acculturation in chapter 8, as well as chapter 3.]

The discovery that the same principle is operative in West Africa, at the southern border of Mohammedan influence, where among the Hausa the pagan *iska* are identified with the *jinn* of the Koran, extends its validity. But if we turn our analysis to Protestant countries, where syncretism of this sort is not possible, we find that though the names of African deities have been but rarely retained, syncretisms take other, more generalized forms. An example of this is the retention of the African requirement of initiation into religious groups through its syncretization with the Christian concept of sanctification

157

achieved through preparation for baptism, or as expressed in the institution of the "mourning ground."

At this point another principle must be stated—that of *reinterpretation*. For where it is not possible to set up syncretisms, the force of cultural conservatism seeks expression in substance, rather than form, in psychological value rather than in name, if the original culture is to survive at all. Here the hypothesis of the importance of resemblance of the old element to the new is again involved. Though to a lesser degree than in the instance of syncretism, reinterpretation also requires that some characteristic of the new cultural element be correlated with a corresponding part of the original one by those to whom it is presented, before the mechanism can operate effectively.

In this fashion, the pattern of polygynous family structure has come to be reinterpreted in terms of successive, rather than of simultaneous plural matings, something which has set in motion an entire train of adjustments. Not the least of these has been the rejection, within the Negro group, of the European interpretation of illegitimacy as applied to offspring of unions not sanctioned by law, and to legal divorce, since these laws are meaningless in terms of aboriginal conventions. The extent to which new orientations of this kind find distribution among Negroes everywhere in the New World demonstrates the effectiveness of the mechanism, not only to achieve cultural but also psychological adaptation to the new setting. This could also be documented from other aspects of culture—economic life, or religion, or music—if considerations of space permitted. Here, however, the example given suffices to illustrate the principle that has been derived.

Retention of original custom under contact, whether through syncretism or reinterpretation is, however, merely one side of the problem, the other being the acceptance of what is newly presented. Here many imponderables enter, the most important being the degree to which outer acceptance involves transfer of values and interpretations in the psychological as well as in the institutional sense. This, of course, raises one of the most difficult problems in the entire field of cultural dynamics—whether any element of culture is ever taken over without some degree of reinterpretation, however free the borrowing.

If this particular question be for the moment disregarded, however, it is to be seen that just as syncretism and reinterpretation are means by which retention of the old is achieved, they are by the same token effective in encouraging the adoption of the new. A succession of matings entered into by a man or woman implies an acceptance of the monogamic principle, at the same time that it points to the method by which, through reinterpretation, the old polygynous tradition has been retained. Where African gods are syncretized with Catholic saints, the significance of the fact that the Negroes, as professing Catholics, have accepted the new religion must not be lost sight of by focusing attention too closely on the retention of aboriginal deities.

When we press the matter, however, we find that the problem is further complicated by the selective nature of borrowing on another level. On the basis of a comparative analysis of African and New World Negro cultures, it is apparent that even under the compulsions of the dominant culture of Whites, Negroes have retained African religious beliefs and practices far more than they have retained economic patterns. But when we examine the patterns of African cultures, we find that there is no activity of everyday living but that it is validated by supernatural sanctions. And consequently, these figure far more in the total life of the people than does any other single facet of the culture such as those matters having to do with making a living, or family structure, or political institutions. This weighting of the concerns of a people constitutes the focus of their culture. *Cultural focus* is thus seen to be that phenomenon which gives a culture its particular emphasis; which permits the outsider to sense its special distinguishing flavor and to characterize its essential orientation in a few phrases.

The role of cultural focus is of such great importance in situations of cultural contact that a further hypothesis may be advanced to the effect that more elements which lie in the area of focus of a receiving culture will be retained than those appertaining to other aspects of the culture, acceptance being greater in those phases of culture further removed from the focal area. Where a culture is under pressure by a dominant group who seek to induce acceptance of its traditions, elements lying in the focal area will be retained longer than those outside it, though in this case retention will of necessity be manifested in syncretisms and reinterpretations.

For example, in the interior of Dutch Guiana, almost the only Europeanisms to be found are those which lie in the realm of material culture. In Brazil, where the Negroes accept most of the dominant European economic order, they adjust to the exigencies of the Church by syncretizing their African deities and continuing to worship them as they are worshipped in Africa. In the United States, where pressures have been most severe, almost no African economic patterns have persisted, but adaptation to Protestantism has been marked by the retention of many Africanisms through reinterpretation.

Still another point that must receive attention has to do with the degree to which elements of a culture that may be peripheral to the focal area, but that ride high in the consciousness of the people— that require thought, or call for decision—are retained under contact when compared to those which, so to speak, are carried below the level of consciousness. These may be termed *cultural imponderables*. Prominent among these are linguistic patterns and musical style, and such sanctions as are comprehended in those determinants of behavior that include types of motor habits, systems of values, or codes of etiquette. Research has demonstrated that manifestations of African culture, wherein there is little conscious awareness, have persisted in the New World to a far greater degree than those cultural elements that lie outside the area of cultural focus. This is not surprising when the factors involved are considered, since the cultural imponderables, being those elements in culture that intrude but slightly upon consciousness are taken for granted, and are thus far more difficult to dislodge from the thought and behavior patterns of individuals subjected to a new culture than those which must be given continuous attention.

Language and musical style may be cited here to illustrate the point. In the case of the former, the analysis of New World Negro dialects in English, French, and Spanish, and their African counterparts in English and French, has shown that the underlying structure of the aboriginal tongues persists longest, and is most resistant to change, while vocabulary and pronunciation exhibit the most non-African elements. But it is just the grammatical configurations of any language that lodge deepest in linguistic habit-patterns, and that present the greatest difficulties where a new language is to be learned—far more so than either phonetics or vocabulary, though this last is easier learned than pronunciation. One does not think about the structure of his speech when he uses his own language; he need only "choose his words," as the saying goes.

Such patterns are laid down very early in life; so that, under contact, they are highly persistent. In like manner it is musical style, the "grammar" of music, that most resists change under contact, so that while music proves to be among the most African elements of Negro culture everywhere, yet in such regions as the United States, or in such a country as Peru, where the retention of Africanisms has been least extensive, the elusive elements of style remain in songs where an aspect such as melodic line has given way to a more European type of musical expression.

On the basis of the findings, then, the hypothesis can be advanced that in situations involving change, cultural imponderables are more resistant than are those elements of which persons are more conscious. It is important to stress in this connection, however, the distinction between this assumption and the hypothesis which holds that material culture is more acceptable under contact than non-material culture. All those phenomena which have been mentioned do fall within the latter category, it is true, but this is incidental to the hypothesis that has been advanced, since the principle is one that concerns process and does not concern form.

An exhaustive treatment of the theoretical basis of Afroamerican research would require the statement of still further hypotheses, dealing with such matters as the effect of population mass, of isolation, and of opportunity for acquiring a new culture, or discussion of the operation of such intangibles as pride in an original culture that is under assault, and a resulting determination to retain it against odds. It would require the evaluation, on the basis of available materials of hypotheses that have been advanced as a result of research in other cultures, or of the more *a priori*, philosophical speculations, such as the principle which correlates a supernaturalistic approach to life with a primitive or rural setting, or that which assumes a special type of mentality for non-European peoples.

Enough hypotheses which have guided Afroamerican research or have developed out of it have been indicated, however, to demonstrate how significant its contribution can be, and indeed, already has been, in furthering the wider ends of the scientific study of man. We have here been concerned with principles that can be applied to culture; we have mentioned one instance where language is to be drawn on; we could, in the same manner, document the point further with reference to the problems of human biology. But whatever the problems to be studied, the advantages presented by the field of Afroamerican studies in the way of breadth of scope and historic control of data, permit assumptions within the field to be tested adequately, before advancing them as applicable to other areas, under differing situations of historical development.

An interesting reinterpretation of an aspect of religion found in Nigeria and in Ghana is the period of seclusion for new devotees observed in Afroamerican cult groups in Haiti, Trinidad, and Brazil. The ceremony—including the symbolic whipping, the reentry into the daily routine, and the "purchasing" of the initiates—is characterized by relaxation and humor. Unlike the large "public" ceremonies in Bahia, Brazil, Herskovits called the panan "a quiet, almost intimate ritual."

7 The Panan, an Afrobahian Religious Rite of Transition *

✛ The rite to be described here is one of a cycle that marks the emergence of novitiates (*yawo*, Yoruba "junior wife") in the Ketu

* Reprinted from *Les Afro-Américains* (Mémoires de l'Institut Français d'Afrique Noire, no. 27) (Dakar: 1953):133–40.

162

sect of Afrobahian cult-groups (*candomblé*) after a period of seclusion wherein they are ritually dedicated to the worship of the gods (*orisha*) by whom they have been chosen. As such, it functions as a mechanism of social reintegration, assuring the initiates that on their return to the daily round they will not be spiritually or physically beset by the dangers arising out of intercourse with the secular world from which they have been withdrawn, and which they are soon to re-enter with new names, as new personalities.

Descriptions of the "public" ceremonies of these cult-groups, especially of the Ketu variety, are numerous and, on the whole, give adequate knowledge of their manifest forms of worship. We have relatively little information, however, as to their integral organization, and less on their complex theology, their inner rituals, or their social functioning. As we probe more deeply into their working, we see emerge a well-defined system of belief that is based on the substantial knowledge of African lore, language, and ritual by officials of the various cult-groups, whose role is accurately described in the local idiom as the *estado-maior*, the "general staff," and on the discipline they enforce in administering the affairs of the group and regulating the behavior of its members. This presence of a clear-cut system is further found in the reasoned understanding and controlled ritual expression of worship on the part of the cult-initiates and other affiliates with various degrees of "understanding" who make up the cult-group. For cult-affiliation, it becomes clear, responds to an hierarchical pattern, stratified on two levels. The first distinguishes the degree of sanctioned participation according to the ritual experience, including the type of offerings, of the individual in relation to his personal god (*eleda*). The second is in accordance with the powers and role assigned to the individual by his *orisha*. The first category determines priorities in participation, the second in direction.

In broadest outline, theology and ritual of all the Afrobahian cult-groups in Bahia, as elsewhere in Brazil, represent well-defined retentions of African worship. A person may become a member in various ways, but can acquire the right of active worship only through initiation. The only exception is the individual who is born in a cult-house while his mother is undergoing training, and becomes an initiate by virtue of having shared the mystic experience *in utero*. The need for initiation—the ultimate degree of participation in cult life— is signalized by the possession of an individual by a deity, who "mounts the head" of the one thus marked as his devotee, and by subsequent divination to determine the name, nature and wishes of the god known as "falling" and "rolling," during the progress of a ceremony at a cult-center. This is directed toward the feet of the priest or priestess of the cult-house (*pai-* or *mãe-de-santo*, or Yoruba *babalorisha* or *iyalorisha*), and toward the quarters which house the novitiates when they are undergoing initiation, the *camarinha*, known by the Gêge (Dahomean) terms *hunko* or *hundemi*, or the Nago (Yoruba) *yara ashe*. In most cases, however, the deity is less exigent and the candidate is permitted to amass the considerable amount of goods and money—considerable, that is, in terms of the prevalent standard of living—that must be in hand to defray the expenses of induction into the cult.

The many cult-groups found in Bahia, and elsewhere in Brazilian centers with an appreciable population of African descent, differ in the degree of their adherence to African religious custom. The most rigorous—"orthodox," in the African sense—are the Gêge, of Dahomean derivation. Most numerous today among those who hold closest to African procedures are the Ketu, who take their designation from the town of the same name lying on the Yoruba-Dahomean border in West Africa. They are essentially Yoruba in derivation and linguistic expression. Another smaller group, the 'Jesha cult, is to be traced to the Yoruba political group of the same name (Ijesha). It may be regarded as a local variation of the generalized Yoruba religious culture that was continued in Bahia. The Nupe, called Tapa, the name even today given them in Africa by the Yoruba, and remnants of the Hausa and their northern and westerly neighbors are incorporated largely into the Ketu group. The Congo-Angola sect, as its name indicates, comes from the more southerly portion of western Africa; its linguistic usages have been traced to Kimbundu, but intensive research, in Brazil, Angola, and western Congo will be necessary before precise provenience can be determined.

The Congo-Angola groups provide the link to the less "orthodox"

Caboclo cults, wherein Indian and Portuguese names of deities abound, wherein Portuguese words are sung to many of the songs, wherein initiatory periods are truncated to a few days or weeks, and wherein the most diverse African and non-African innovations are present. Finally the continuum moves to the Spiritualist groups, and to full-blown European beliefs and practices, many of which are syncretized into even the most "orthodox" aggregates. In a sense, this completes the circle, and makes for the cultural integration of Afrobahian religious life that is the outer form of the inner unities of belief and value systems that give the Afrobahian the psychological adjustment seen in his relations with his fellows, with those of other social classes, and with the universe in which he lives his life.

The *panan* (or *pana*, without nasalization), essentially comprises a series of major rituals, each of which symbolically reproduces some act which the emergent initiate will perform in daily life. Because, as in West Africa, these initiates are in great majority women—in the rite described here, there were no male initiates—most of the acts symbolized pertain to the woman's sphere of life. In performing these acts, the initiate brings into play a protective force that comes from anticipating unwitting transgression of ritual prescription, while at the same time re-introducing this newly-born personality—in a spiritual sense—to the world in which life must be lived.

Unlike the great "public" ceremonies, the *panan* is a quiet, almost intimate ritual. At the one to be described there were no more than twenty-five or thirty spectators, many of them officiating members of the cult-group holding the rite, the others relatives of the initiates. The contrast of this with the elaborate ceremony of name-giving, shortly before, marking the initial emergence of these same initiates from their seclusion, publicly demonstrating their skill in dancing for their gods, and showing their rich ceremonial paraphernalia, could not have been greater. No general announcement of smaller rituals of this sort is made, as is done for the "public" dances. For while the *panan* is in no way to be regarded as one of the esoteric elements of the initiatory cycle, of which there are many, an outsider, unless he were a friend of the priest or of the family of an initiate, and his interest in these matters was recognized, would never know of its occurrence. Yet in its relaxation, its humor, its quality as theater, it helps us understand some of the intangible reasons why African cult practices have been retained so tenaciously in this portion of the New World.

. . .

At 9:45,[1] all being in readiness, the *yawos* filed in and stood, heads bent, in a row before a bench that had been placed along the wall of the *barracão*, the large room where the public ceremonies take place. The priest, holding each in turn by the shoulders, lowered and raised her three times before finally seating her. Then first the priest, and after him in turn the assistant priestess, (the *mãe pequena;* Yoruba *iyakekere*) and a younger woman, wearing a plain white dress, later identified as the named successor of the *mãe pequena*, first took up a switch lying at hand for the purpose, then a *palmatória*—an instrument of wood with holes bored in its flat surface that was used to chastise slaves by striking them on the palm of the hands—and a broken china dish. With the switch, each of the *yawos* was symbolically whipped on shoulders, arms and legs; her hands were struck twice with the *palmatória;* and from the dish some dust was scraped off with a stone and made to fall on her head. The significance of the whip, called *atori de Oshala*, was explained by the priest in a short homily. If in the future, he said, these initiates do not obey those who rank them, saying when they are called on to perform a task for their *orisha* that they will not do it, that they are too busy, or that they cannot, then they will be punished by Oshala who, as father of the gods, is the one who more than any of the other African deities chastises those who disobey. And when the *mãe pequena* used the whip on the two initiates for Yansan, the goddess of the wind, she prefaced her statement about the need for obedience to one of them with the phrase "as you know already." The *palmatória* similarly sig-

[1] Eighth of February, 1942. It was one of the many rituals, public and private, attended in various cult-houses during field research carried on in Bahia and elsewhere in Brazil, under a grant from the Rockefeller Foundation, that occupied a period of 12 months in 1941–1942.

nified that punishment would be meted out to those who disobeyed; but the significance of the grains of dust from the broken dish was not indicated. However, it was thrown, crashing, to the ground after it had been used.

When this episode was finished, the priest called the senior initiate of the cult-group, an elderly woman, who repeated the symbolic whipping and palmstriking on each of the *yawos*, and after her all other women who were present were summoned to perform the same acts. As each woman went forward, she put a coin in a plate placed on the ground for the purpose; in one case, where a woman had no money, the priest himself gave her a coin to put in it. The *mãe pequena* then concluded with a quick repetition of the two ritual acts in the name of five women who could not themselves perform them. One wore a black skirt, and hence could not approach the newly initiated *yawos* whose spiritual condition was still precarious, wearing the color of death, while the others were caring for infants and could not be disturbed. It was then the turn of the men. First the chief *ogan* of the group performed the symbolic acts, then a man, an *ogan* of another center, his guest, then an elderly white-haired man, the father of one of the *yawos*, and then some ten or twelve others present. This concluded the first episode, which took just under an hour to complete.

The second part, which began at 10:40, symbolized the re-entry of the initiates into activities of everyday life. The priest again pointed the lesson of the symbolism—that each initiate must perform each of these tasks since, if this were not done, harm might come to her when she later had to do them. The order of the tasks, and the manner in which they were performed, follow:

(1) Along one wall of the room stood a row of water-jars, one for each initiate. Each jar was covered with a cloth, which the *yawo* who used it made into a head-pad, putting the jar on her head. Then, in a line, the group went outside the *barracão* "to get water." In several minutes they returned with the pots upright; each "poured" the imaginary water into a tin container, and put the jar down.

(2) Each took the broom that was standing ready, and swept a part of the floor.

167

(3) Each went through the pantomime of "pouring water" from the container into a basin, and then "washed" the cloth that had been used for a head-pad.

(4) At the center of the hall was a table, an iron standing ready on the floor nearby. Each woman, in turn, went to the table and, taking up the iron, which was cold, went through the pantomime of "ironing" her cloth. It was a commentary on the differing personalities of the *yawos* to see how differently each went about the task in hand. All of them, however, gave a creditable performance, in a light, humorous vein, but without exaggerated caricature or exhibitionism.

(5) A coal-pot, some coals, a grate and a fire-fan were brought forward. Each *yawo* lighted a match, applied it to the coals, and fanned the "fire."

(6) A pot was then put on the "fire," and each initiate, using the stirring spoon in it, proceeded to "cook" and "season" her dish.

(7) A mortar and pestle was used by each. The pounded "meal" of cassava or beans was placed in a woven sifter and "sifted" into a basin.

(8) Each initiate worked at a grinding stone.

(9) A basin of water was placed on the table, containing two leaves, each leaf symbolizing a fish. The *yawos*, in turn, using the knife ready at hand, "cleaned" the "fish." One of them, with a sense of theatre, added a realistic touch by snipping off the "tail"—that is, by cutting off the stem of the leaf. All this went on to the accompaniment of much laughter from the audience, and an impassive seriousness of the *yawo*.

It was now 11:05, and the *yawos* were again seated on their bench. The next two episodes represented acts that are taboo for an initiate, and for which immunity must be had if later done, even unknowingly.

(10) A candle was lighted, and after it had been passed behind the head of each initiate, she blew it out.

(11) Lighting a cigarette, a young man blew smoke in the face of each *yawo*.

The women then arose from their places, and, forming a line, filed outside the *barracão*. The following items were next enacted:

(12) As each initiate re-entered the hall, she simulated buying at a market.

(13) She took an incense-burner, and went about the room with it, making motions as though to distribute the smoke in the manner of purifying the hall with incense.

(14) A tray of fruit was brought in, and each *yawo* put it on her head, going out of the door and back and about the hall, hawking her wares. This was a further source of great amusement, since each initiate tried to be as imaginative as possible in naming what she had to "sell."

(15) In the meantime, on the other side of the room, the *yawos* went to grate leaves on a grater—this was "grating coconuts."

(16) Simultaneously, nearby, others were now mashing leaves in a basin, representing the preparation of the seasoning for dishes to be cooked.

(17) A ladder was placed near a window. Each *yawo* climbed it to call to an imaginary trader outside to come and bring his wares— again, with imagination in what was said, and much laughter from the audience.

(18) The initiates then went outside once more, and, despite the full skirts that each wore, climbed over the window-sill and into the hall. One or two of the women had to be helped in this, an incident that the spectators punctuated with comment and laughter.

(19) Now they made themselves ready to go out. On the settee were comb, brush, powder, mirror and other feminine accessories, and each took her turn at using them.

(20) Next each woman went over to the dish in which offerings of coins had been placed, and "counted" what was there. Each announced her "findings" in fantastic figures, with simulated high seriousness, to the delight of the spectators.

The time was now 11:20, which gives some indication of the celerity and smoothness with which the items in the program of events succeeded each other. The next group of episodes, that continued without pause, concerned still other phases of life:

(21) The shoes of the initiates had been brought into the hall

169

some time previously, and each *yawo* now got into hers. This proved to be somewhat difficult, since, as the priest remarked, "Your feet are large," and in actuality must have spread during the period of seclusion, when none had been worn. This was a part of a series of preparatory acts that symbolized getting ready to go to Mass [2] and continued with gestures putting on of bracelets and other ornaments. A woman came out holding three comic looking hats, which three of the initiates put on; then she handed them three books which represented missals. There was great laughter again as the three, caricaturing elegance at every step, walked a short distance out of the door on their "way to mass," to be followed by the remaining group of initiates who repeated the act—three *yawos*, then three more, then the remaining two.

(22) The next episode to be "experienced" was "getting married." The priest went off to a small chapel, of the type found in all cult-centers, which in this case was then in a nearby house of the complex of cult buildings. These chapels, in appearance at least, do not differ from any private Catholic altar, with a small figure of the patron saint of the establishment—in this case, Saint Anthony, syncretized with the African deity Ogun, the *orisha* of the founder of the cult-house. This episode had as its aim to ensure that the *yawos* would find happiness in the relationships that had been interrupted when they went into seclusion, and were to be re-entered, or that were later to be formed. The episode, it should be indicated, not only included the taking of the vows but simulated the performance of the sexual act, the "groom" in each case being represented by a male infant. It is to be noted that when a small boy of about five years of age was brought forward to act in this capacity, he was rejected by those in charge as being "too old." The *yawos* went off to the chapel two at a time, and the bell could be heard ringing to "celebrate" the "marriage." When they returned, each "groom" was carried by his mother, while each "bride" had flowers. The "couple" then lay down

---

[2] As has been demonstrated by all students of these cults, the members are simultaneously worshippers of the African gods and communicants of the Catholic Church. It is from this fact that some of the most significant syncretic aspects of Afrobrazilian cultural adjustments arise.

on a sleeping-mat that had been placed for the purpose, and were covered with a cloth for a moment before the *yawo* got up and the infant was taken away. The audience was especially diverted by the first "groom," aged perhaps two years, who disliked the entire performance and made vocal his protest.

The "marriage" over, the succeeding episodes concerned behavior inside the home, where the initiate was presumably mistress of a prosperous house.

(23) Each initiate took her turn at hammering a nail.

(24) Each took a small piece of cloth, cut it a bit and sewed a few stitches.

(25) A meat-grinder was given a few turns by each.

(26) Each turned a few pages of a cheap magazine as though reading it.

(27) A dust cloth was used.

(28) Each put up an umbrella.

(29) Each brushed her clothes.

(30) The radio was turned on and, as the *yawos* listened for a moment, some short-wave station was heard.

It was now 11:45, and from the interior of the building adjoining the *barracão* came the sound of voices, and some music. The *yawos* stood about, waiting until the table was set for the final episode.

(31) The senior initiate of the cult-house, acting as hostess, cut the meat that had been brought, and put a piece on each plate. The *yawos* then took their places, to simulate partaking of a "formal" meal. They ate the meat; then bread was passed. Their manners were excellent, and their comportment was watched with interest by all those present. A young man, as "waiter," poured a little wine for each, which each drank, first holding up her glass and pronouncing the polite "Licença" before drinking. Each drank a little water, and then partook of dessert, which consisted of small cakes. Finally all arose, and once more took their places on the bench.

At midnight a five minute interval ensued, after which the priest announced that they would proceed to the ceremony of "purchasing" the *yawos*. He pointed to each, asking who would "buy" them. One had a father, one a husband as "purchasers"; one was named as a

171

"slave of Ogun." This may have had one of two meanings—that she had been "purchased" by an *ogan*, a member of the cult-group, for the deity, or that she "redeemed" herself. The other initiates seemed to have no one to "purchase" them; whereupon the priest asked "How much are the *yawos* worth?" and forthwith announced prices, which would either have to be paid by a future "purchaser," or paid by the initiate herself over a period of time. Though actual money passes when these "purchases" are made, the obligations assumed in the ensuing relationship between the "purchaser" and the *yawo* make for a complex of reciprocal obligations, much of which is ritual in character. The prices announced for devotees of the various deities were as follows; for those vowed to Yansan, the god of the wind, 400$000, for those of Ogun, Oshala and Oshosi, the gods of iron and war, the sky and the hunt, respectively, 350$000, those for Oshun and Omolu, the deities of fresh water and of the earth, 300$000.[3]

Without waiting for further bidding or permitting conversation, the priest went on to the closing episode, the benediction. A mat was put down and, beginning with the "slave" of Ogun, each *yawo* prostrated herself individually in turn before him, kissing his hands, and then the hands of the younger woman who was to be the future *mãe pequena*. The mat was then transferred to the opposite side of the hall, near the spectators, so that all might receive blessings. The collection plate was put down at the head of the line which the new initiates now formed, and as each spectator passed down this line to receive the blessings bestowed, he placed a contribution in it. The chief *ogun* was first to be blessed, after putting a note for 100$000 in the upturned hands of the first initiate; then two other *oguns*; the other male spectators, followed by the women who were present, and then the children. Contributions were generous in terms of accepted values, with more than 250$000 in the plate by the time the children went down the line of initiates to be blessed. The blessing itself consisted in having the hand kissed by each *yawo*; and to simply make a contribution was not regarded as sufficient, as was seen in the rebuke

[3] At the time of this research, the unit of currency in Brazil was the *milreis*, now termed *cruzeiro*. One of these units (1$000) has the value of five United States cents, or about thirty French francs.

172

administered by the priest to one spectator who hesitated at participating in this aspect of the rite.

The ceremony ended at 12:45 A.M.. The *yawos* returned to their
living quarters to await the next rite that would bring them one step
nearer the resumption of everyday life as full-fledged initiates. Spectators and cult-members went about exchanging greetings. . . .

*The use of divination to diagnose the causes of illnesses
and other misfortunes, to predict the future, and to discover the
wishes and attitudes of the gods, is worldwide. African, European,
American Indian, and East Indian divinatory practices have often
been syncretized in some parts of the New World. In Paramaribo,
Surinam, the Herskovitses found that American Indian, Negro, and
white magic are ranked in strength according to the situation requiring attention.*

8   Divination in Paramaribo, Surinam *

✤ The references we have made to divining must already have
suggested that divination plays an important part in the life of the
Suriname town Negroes. Indeed, so impressed are the Paramaribo
Negroes themselves with this, that those who have knowledge of the
life of the Saramacca tribe of Bush-Negroes make the point that there
is greater recourse to divination in the city than in the bush. It was
claimed that among the Saramacca people there are only a few important diviners to be found—one at the village of *Lombe,* a short
distance south of the rail-head, and several others in the distant village
of *Dahome,* on the far upper river—whereas in Paramaribo alone,
there are several times as many, and they are the more skilled. While
to our own knowledge of life in the Suriname bush this statement is

* Reprinted from M. J. and F. S. Herskovits, *Suriname Folk-lore,* pp. 55–59
(New York: Columbia University Press, 1936).

not borne out by actual fact, the significance of such an assertion as demonstrating the place the Suriname town Negroes give their own diviners—despite the superiority ordinarily acceded the Bush-Negroes in dealing with the supernatural—is of the first order.

Diviners are called *lukuman,* "those who look." Loosely, however, all those who deal with the supernatural, whether as diviners or as workers of evil magic, or as providers of magic which protects, as well as those who exorcise evil spirits such as ghosts, and those who pacify personal spirits which have been aroused, are called *Djuka.* Another name, with the same general implication, is *bonu,*[1] a third *obiaman.* Conversationally, a practitioner of any one of the above categories is also referred to as a *wintiman,* or a *wisiman.* When, however, an individual informant is questioned closely, he carefully differentiates these categories. A *lukuman,* he explains, is a diviner who also cures souls. A *wintiman* is one who deals with the spirits called *winti,* the gods, and cures all illnesses sent by these spirits. A *wisiman* is a practitioner of black magic, and as such can if he chooses also cure black magic. The maker of protective charms, if yet finer differentiation is sought, is the *obiaman,* one who deals in *obia,*[2] and the *obiaman* will also at times be designated as the one who cures *wisi,* evil magic. It must be indicated, nevertheless, that in reality this separation of function is most frequently only theoretical, for it is seldom that a man in any one of the categories named is not competent as well in at least one other, and some are skilled in all.

While discussing divination and those who divine, it is also necessary to name the Indian *piaiman,* and the *kartaman*—literally "card-man"—the latter of whom may be White or Javanese or Hindu as well as Negro. In order to understand why the Negro values the

[1] *Bonu* has, as its derivation, the Fon term *gbo,* a Dahomean word applied to magical charms.

[2] According to the suggestion of Professor D. Westermann, the word *obia* may be derived from the *Bia* river, a mythologically important river of the Gold Coast, conceived by the Twi-speaking peoples as a brother of *Tano,* the god of all rivers. The prefix "o" denotes the singular in Twi. Another possible derivation may be from the Efik word *'Mbian* while Sir H. H. Johnstone states "*Obia* seems to be a variant or a corruption of an Efik or Ibo word from the northeast or east of the Niger delta, which simply means 'Doctor.' " Recently Williams has advanced the theory that the word is to be derived from the Twi *obayifo.*

Indian diviner, we must glance at his attitude toward the ranking of Indian, Negro, and White supernatural powers. The logic with which he approaches this problem is that for himself his own magic—Negro magic—is the strongest, but that, in certain situations, the magic of the Indian takes precedence over his own, because the Indians, as the autochthonous inhabitants of the land, have the greatest control over the spirits of earth and water. Of White man's magic, the reading of the future by means of cards has some vogue, and anyone, whether White, Hindu, or Javanese, who can tell fortunes with cards, is said to use the White man's method of divining.

When questioning the soul, the answers are given by the tilting of a cup containing water and an egg which rests on the head of the person whose soul is being called, or by the tilting of a cup or bowl, also containing water and an egg, held in the right hand. In both these instances, the diviner uses a folded mat, but sometimes the mat alone is employed. A *lukuman* may also look into a mirror when he reads the future, or he may watch the surface of a basin of water which stands before him, and when the water becomes troubled the spirit is said to have entered it, and the questioning proceeds as it does when the cup placed on the head or held in the hand begins to shake. In all those instances where a mat or its equivalent, a fan, or water in a basin, is used, the answers can only be "yes," or "no." Divining, however, may be done by means of calling upon a *winti* to enter into the body of either the diviner or of the person who came to consult him, and causing this *winti* to speak. Albinos, and those exhibiting strains of albinism, who are called *bonkoru*,[3] are particularly gifted diviners for they are all said to have strong *winti*, and consequently important remedies.[4] If the *winti* is one of African or Indian origin, it is said to "speak tongues," and only the *wintiman*—the priest or priestess—is

[3] Among the Saramacca people albinos are called *Tone* people, that is, they belong to the river gods. In Dahomey such people are said to be sacred to *Lisa*, god of the sun.
[4] An informant told of one such remedy that had restored his own health, which consisted of herbs gathered by his mother in the bush, while her moves to pluck now one, now another, were directed by the *winti* of the diviner who, in his own home in the city, sat in a state of possession, shaking a rattle and chanting.

175

able to interpret what is said by the spirit. Certain generalized methods of divination may be mentioned here in passing, which, though they do not need a specialist to perform, may also be employed by a specialist. Thus, a fowl which is being sacrificed either to an individual's *akra* or to a *winti*, is opened and its intestines or testicles are examined to see whether they are white or discolored. If they are white, the omen is one of good luck, while if they are not, the prediction is bad luck. The same test is also used as an ordeal to establish the innocence of a woman who disclaims guilt in adultery. Again, those who are possessed of *Ingi winti* (Indian spirits), especially the water-Indian spirits, are thought to have the gift of divination, even when they are not specialists in the sense that the *lukuman* is a specialist. Certain individuals, as well, at whose birth abnormal phenomena were manifest, such as a caul, or a navel cord entwined about the neck, are thought to have special aptitudes for divination and magical practice. Such persons are encouraged to go through specialized training with an established diviner to fit themselves for this profession.

Divination as practiced by the specialist, then, is a matter of training. The knowledge of the technique passes, in the main, from a man to his brother until, the generation exhausted, it is given to one of their sisters' sons. The one chosen is either selected because he is specially intelligent, or because by divination, or in a dream, he is discovered to have special aptitude for the profession. If a father cares, however, he may teach his own son his craft. In the case of women, the knowledge is passed on to sisters, or one of a woman's own daughters or sons; or if a woman has no children, then to the children of a sister. The rule is that the technique of a man is taught to a man, and that of a woman to a woman. It must be made clear that we found no sex division in the types of divination employed by diviners of the two sexes. General practice is to choose a male *lukuman* for illnesses of the soul, but for ills caused by the *winti*, a man or woman practitioner may be selected. There is a way of becoming a *lukuman* other than by inheriting the knowledge and this occurs when an African *komfo* [5] decides to take possession of a man or a woman who has been chosen by him as his fitting medium. It is

[5] Komfo is the Ashanti-Fanti word for priest.

not necessary that this *komfo*-spirit should have manifested itself actively to the family before. In our ensuing discussion of *winti,* we shall see how certain important spirits are sent to reside in trees and stones by those who die without successors, or whose successors are unwilling to continue the worship of the African gods. It may be that one such spirit who, while remaining quiescent, had yet continued to identify himself with the family, might cause a man or woman to go into a state of possession, and reveal the answers to questions sought of the supernatural. Such a *komfo* needs, to be sure, to prove himself, but once his reputation for curing and prophesying [6] is established, he is then said to *"wroko furu moni*—earn much money"—for his possessor.

An illness may be caused by violating a *trefu* [food taboo]. Perhaps it is an unconscious violation, arising out of the fact that a man's mother had never told him the name of his true father, and consequently he had been observing food taboos which were not his own and had been neglecting to observe those which were his, since these personal food taboos are inherited from the father. The *lukuman* is consulted, and he both diagnoses the cause of the illness, and names the foods to be avoided. A person's illnesses or difficulties which bring him to the diviner may arise out of a violation of the injunctions of some deity. He may have urinated in that portion of the yard that is identified as the habitat of the *Gron Mama*—Earth Mother—of that particular yard. Or a person may come to the *lukuman* because he has found a bundle containing porcupine-quills under his door-step, or one of red and blue cotton, or a broken calabash with evil-smelling weeds, soiled cloth and thorny bits of wood in it, and these, he knows, bode him no good. A man consults the *lukuman* to discover why his rice-crop does not prosper, or he comes to find out who is responsible for a recent accidental death in his family that is suspected to have been brought about by other than natural causes. In the last instance, he waits until after the eighth-day wake has been celebrated, and then

[6] An especially valued instrument is called "the *komfo* telephone," whose "strong name" is *Kausi.* It is a stick, magically treated, which if concealed in a room, records all that is spoken, and if it is but sprayed with rum and made to hear the proper formula, need only to have one end of it placed against the ear to repeat what it had recorded.

goes to the *lukuman* to have him divine the person who had invoked black magic to cause the death of his relative. Or it may be such an incident as was related to us, where a *Yorka*—a ghost—has manifested itself, and, through this manifestation, presages trouble.

This incident concerns a man who was sitting one night (about a week before he told us of the occurrence), drinking beer with some friends.

He left the table for a few moments, and when he returned, his friends said they had seen a white hand reach out for his glass. When he looked, the glass was not there. He had laughed about it, but had told his mother.[7]

Herskovits' study of "voodoo" (vodun) helped to dispel the idea that Haitian peasant religion consists of a fantastic set of beliefs and rites. The worshippers understand their obligations to the gods; good fortune or bad comes from the fulfillment or the avoidance of these duties. Herskovits was one of the first social scientists to recognize the socially normal nature of spirit possession and the rules which govern it (1937b, p. 148). Haitian vodun, like santeria in Cuba, and shango in Brazil and in Trinidad, combines elements of West African traditional religions with Catholicism. These syncretistic religious cults are fascinating instances of acculturation among New World Negroes.

9 What Is "Voodoo"? *

✤ More than any other single term, the word "voodoo" is called to mind whenever mention is made of Haiti. Conceived as a grim sys-

---

[7] The informant's comment at this point carries some significance in terms of acculturation: "All my mother does is go to church. She don't want me to go to *winti*-dances, even to look. But if anything happens, she runs to a *lukuman*."

* Abridged from chapter 8 of Herskovits' *Life in a Haitian Valley* (New York: Knopf, 1937).

tem of African practices, it has come to be identified with fantastic rites and to serve as a symbol of daring excursions into the esoteric. Its dark mysteries have been so stressed that it has become customary to think of the Haitians as living in a universe of psychological terror.

What, then, is "voodoo"? "Voodoo," or Vodun, as it will be termed here, following native pronunciation, is a complex of African belief and ritual governing in large measure the religious life of the Haitian peasantry.

In Dahomey, the ancient West African kingdom whence the term has come, Vodun means "god" and is a general name for all deities. This source of the word has long been known. For instance, M. L. E. Moreau de St.-Mery, in his work *Description topographique, physique, civile, et historique de la partie française de l'Isle Saint-Domingue* (Philadelphia, 1797 and 1798), wrote:

"According to the Arada Negroes, the real followers of Vaudaux in the colony . . . *Vaudaux* signifies an all powerful and super-natural being on which depend all the events that come to pass on this globe."

Two historical facts must be kept constantly in mind. The first is that Vodun derives from a background of African theology and ceremonialism. The second is that Haiti's Negroes have continuously been subjected to the influence of Catholicism during the centuries that have passed since their introduction into the island.

Yet another point may prove suggestive in providing a useful point of view for an analysis of the Vodun cult. This bears upon a difficulty, impossible and happily unnecessary to resolve, in the field study of religion. This difficulty arises out of the degree of variation in answers to questions dealing with the same point. These answers differ not only according to the status of the individual in the cult, since layman and priest have understandably different concepts of the functions of deities based on unequal degrees of expert knowledge, but the extent to which an individual has religious interests or is indifferent to them influences the nature of his responses.

A fundamental fallacy results from the fact that except where there is an official sanctioned theology—which makes for dogma, and often for perfunctory worship, in contrast with the living dynamic nature of Haitian peasant belief and ritual—there are no "real" answers to questions in the field of religion. The student pursuing the "correct" statement will find that, no matter how painstaking his method and how extensive his precautions, the versions of different persons can never be entirely reconciled, unless a false appearance of truth is given to his findings.

If the underlying philosophy of the universe held by the Haitian is summarized, as it can be abstracted from his expressions of belief and from his observed behavior, this philosophy might be phrased somewhat as follows: The ruler of the universe is God, its Creator, who shares this task with His son Jesus, the saints of the Church, and the Holy Ghost. Man has been endowed with a soul, and the soul, which has come from God, returns to God for judgment and, if necessary, for punishments at the end of its sojourn on earth.

From Africa—*Guinée*—the Negroes brought other deities, termed variously *loa*, *mystères*, or *saints*, and these deities have been inherited through succeeding generations by the descendants of those who brought them to Haiti. The specific function of the African spirits in the Haitian system was given in the following terms by one of their devotees:

"The loa are occupied with men, their task is to cure. They can make a person work better than he otherwise would. When the loa possess people, they give helpful advice. But they cannot do the things that God does. They can protect a garden, but they cannot make a garden grow, for streams, rain and thunder come from God."

Another statement clearly shows the same concept: "God made the loa, but did not make them so they might do evil. When a man purchases a loa for money, that spirit will do evil as well as good, but God becames angry and will not accept these bad spirits into the sky, and He drives them away."

The most striking element in the Vodun cult is the manner in which the gods are said to "possess" their devotees. Despite the fact that this is the aspect of Haitian religion that seems to the casual observer its least restrained and least disciplined, possession occurs according to well-defined rules and under specifically defined circumstances.

When a person is possessed for the first time, the spirit which is said to animate him is known as a *loa bossal*, an "untamed" god. The word *bossal*, which in the early days was applied to newly arrived Africans, has always been a term of contumely, and today the same feeling-tone is continued through the belief that since all things in the universe are subject to observable regulation, and animals and plants and human beings must all live according to these rules, the loa, as members of society, may not manifest the unrestrained and often dangerous traits of unpredictable behavior which characterize them before they have been "baptized" and thus brought under proper control.

Baptism of a deity most often occurs when a boy or girl is possessed by a family loa, especially if it is one which gives that knowledge of healing and divination meant by the word *connaissance*. Sometimes, though not always, this possession is violent, and the prospective devotee rages about the house, destroying whatever comes to hand. On occasion, since custom frowns on possession at a ceremony not given by the family of the one possessed, possessions of this kind mean either that the loa need baptism; or that, being baptized, its devotee has been negligent in serving the god.

No actual rite of baptism of a loa—or, as it is also termed, of *lavé tête*, "washing the head"—was witnessed by this writer, but the account of the ceremony given here, obtained independently from several persons, represents an adequate exposition of the rite as performed in the town of Mirebalais. A room is prepared where the person whose loa is to be baptized must remain for three days. The mat or bed on which the neophyte rests is covered with fresh sheets and pillow-cases, and three changes of clothing are made ready, one of which must be entirely new for the last day of the ceremony. These are in the color of the god being "baptized"; that is, if the loa were revealed to be such a one as Damballa, Aida Wedo, or Gran' Erzilie, everything would be white, but if it were Gran' Siligbo, the colors would be blue and white; if Ogun, everything would be red; if Ossange, blue; where the god is one of the Pétro suite, such as 'Ti Kita or Bosu, everything would be black.

During the three days' "retreat" the one whose loa is being consecrated lies alone. All day long the men and women of the family sit in the next room or outside the house, singing and praying, though at night they sleep, since "this is not a wake." They not only sing the songs sacred to the loa being baptized, but also the canticles of the Virgin, while prayers of the Church are recited under the leadership of the *prêt' savanne*, the "bush-priest" whose ability to read the prayers makes him an essential figure in all Vodun rites. They may from time to time have "a little procession" about the room where the novitiate lies, when small banners in the color of the god are carried. Soft drinks and a *mangé sec*—a "dry" offering—are given the god, and white tapers and an oil lamp are lighted. Chicken and rice may also be cooked for any god except Gede, while chocolate and rice with milk are favored, since it is said "the loa loves desserts"—a commentary on the very immediate and human character of these spirits.

The actual baptism, or "washing of the head," is performed on the third day of the ceremony by a Vodun priest or priests who is a member of the family, though any member who has important loa and the necessary *connaissance* may officiate if the membership of the family includes no priest. As at any baptism, there must be a godfather and godmother, and preference is given those who are the parents of twins or are themselves twins. The officiant must be possessed at the time, since, it is said, "one loa baptizes another."

Leaves of the basilique tree are steeped in perfumed cold water, and the hands of the one who baptizes are first immersed in the liquid; then, while songs of the loa and canticles of the Virgin are sung, he washes the head of the person to be baptized. Possession occurs immediately, and the new devotee lies back, half conscious, while all others kneel, seeking word from the loa to learn if it is satisfied. If an affirmative answer is given, all retire, the person possessed remaining in the room to sleep through the night. A "ball," but not a Vodun dance, may celebrate the event either the next day or later, but this is not obligatory, and most often those present, after eating, quietly disperse.

The following day, the one who has been baptized goes to the family place of worship and greets those who have helped him. Only one further rite is necessary, and this solely when the loa bossal is revealed to be a hostile god. Then the loa, after having been baptized, is "restrained" by being placed in a jar and buried, so it cannot later emerge and trouble the family of the one to whom it has come.

To have a baptized loa merely means that the worship of the loa is thereafter carried on in regular form. The worshipper learns how to *marré*, or "tie" his spirit, so as to enjoy the social aspects of a Vodun dance without fear that his loa will come unbidden. He gives it small offerings from time to time, and if it becomes insistent, or if his family is being troubled by its gods, he takes full part in the rituals that are staged.

In native idiom, a person when possessed is "mounted" by his god, and thereafter becomes his *ch'wal*, or "horse." A devotee may come under the influence of a number of spirits during a single ceremony or dance, one loa succeeding another. The first deity that ever came to a person, however, for him constitutes the chief of his gods—his *mait' tête*—and the leader of any deities which may subsequently possess him. It is this loa alone that is "baptized," and this one alone "taken from his head" at his death; and, as far as he is concerned, all his other gods are under the control of this *mait tête*, so that any agreement which he may enter into with this principal spirit must be respected by all the others.

Fundamentally, to be possessed by a loa means that an individual's spirit is literally dispossessed by that of the god. Personalities undergo radical change in accordance with the nature of the deity, while even the sex of the one possessed is disregarded if it differs from that of the god, so that, for example, a woman "mounted" by Ogun is always addressed as Papa Ogun. One wears the colors of the god and the ornaments he likes, eating and drinking those things he prefers, and otherwise manifesting his peculiar characteristics—rolling on the earth, if possessed by Damballa or chattering incessantly if by Gede.

Not everyone, by any means, is subject to states of possession. If the existence of individual differences in the capacity for religious expression is recognized, it becomes apparent that while some react to the supernatural with immediate and overwhelming emotion, and others, though incapable of as deep a response, do sense the mysteries of possession, there are still others who go through life without ever feeling this religious "thrill." In native explanation, it is the former to whom the gods manifest themselves, who become the *ch'wal* of their loa; while to the latter the deities never make themselves known.

Scientifically, the phenomenon of possession in Negro cultures, at least, is as yet unsatisfactorily explained, largely because of the almost complete absence of adequate reports on the background and incidence of specific cases. Perhaps the most satisfactory approach to its understanding is through a consideration of it in terms of differences in nervous instability, which may be thought of as predisposing different persons to experience the religious thrill in different degrees; or, in other terms, by reference to their differing susceptibility to suggestion.

One must reject an hypothesis which attempts to explain the Vodun of Haiti in terms of the neuroses, even when, as in the admirable exposition of Dr. J. C. Dorsainvil in *Vodou et Névrose* (Port-au-Prince, 1931), the approach neglects neither accepted genetic theory in stressing the inheritance of neurotic tendencies in voduist family lines, nor the important historical forces which have been operative. For in terms of the patterns of Haitian religion, possession is not abnormal, but normal; it is set in its cultural mold as are all other phases of conventional living. That it gives release from psychic tension does not alter the case; neither does the fact that it offers a way to the satisfaction of unfulfilled desires, as when the god, speaking through a woman under possession, demands a necklace or bracelet which, though forever the property of the god, will be worn by his devotee.

These facts merely emphasize the compensatory character of the phenomenon. The social situation of the individual also enters; some undoubtedly simulate possession for the attention it brings them, while a person who experiences no serious difficulties in the course of his life is perhaps never called upon to ask whether or not he is properly serving his gods; is never placed in a situation for which possession would be a release. Hence to consider all possession as something which falls within the range of psychopathology is to approach it handicapped by a fundamental misconception.

The best evidence of the socially normal nature of possession is the existence of rules governing its incidence which are well understood by all. Not everyone who is a *ch'wal* may become possessed at any dance or *service,* for the gods, if properly under control, are permitted to come only to members of the family giving the rite. If a loa persists in dancing at a Vodun dance given by another family, it is either one of these loa bossal already described, or a loa *vagabond,* and may be scolded by the *hungan:* "You must not come here! You are not wanted! Go home where you belong!"

The passion with which a person resists his god, when he feels possession coming on at a rite not given by his own family, is particularly instructive. Men have been seen holding so tightly to the rafters of the shelter under which the dance was being held that the muscles of their forearms formed great cords, while beads of perspiration rolled down their foreheads. A person who must live away from his family for a long time usually takes steps to "feed" his loa in order to satisfy it, for it is more important to give offerings to the spirits than to dance for them. He therefore either quietly prepares a sacrifice of cereals and liquor in his own room or sends money home so that his loa may be "fed" at the family habitation, and his absence explained to it.

When Vodun deities are discussed in Mirebalais, most often two "companies" of them are mentioned, the Rada and the Pétro "squads." In one list of gods that was obtained, the word *Rada,* derived from the name of the ancient principality of Allada in Dahomey, called forth the explanation *"qui veut dire Dahomey"*—"which is to say, Dahomey," though it should be made clear that neither the words *Rada* nor *Dahomey* are any longer recognized in Haiti as place-names, being today simply qualifying designations of *loa.* There are regional differences in the number and ranking of other categories of gods that hold no important place in Mirebalais. The existence of these other categories is, of course, well known, and one person referred to "the seventeen and twenty-one classes of *loa,*" of

185

which, however, only the following were named: Rada, Pétro, Dahomey, Guinée, Congo, Nago, Ibo, and Wangol. Of these the Congo and the Ibo gods are well known, though their worship is chiefly restricted to individual families, while the Nago and Dahomey categories are most commonly grouped under the term *Rada*. Guinée is often understood as a general designation for all *loa* outside the Rada, Nago, Congo, and Ibo groupings and for certain Pétro gods. Wangol derives from the geographical entity Angola.

From comparatively early times the impression has been given that certain of these classes of gods perform only good, and others evil. Nothing could be further from the truth than this attempt to read European concept into Haitian ideology, for though some gods are feared far more than others, and some generally regarded with affection, even these latter bring great harm to a neglectful devotee, while the gods whose power validates the most malignant magic may, in certain situations, work for the good of their worshippers.

A general principle in the cult of the dead is that in the normal course of events those who die deliver up their souls to God, making the care for these souls primarily a concern of the Church, but it is recognized that there are others who become loa. This occurs when an individual, usually a priest or priestess of the Vodun cult, who during his lifetime was known to possess great supernatural power, dies without having had his loa "withdrawn from his head." Burdened by these spirits, and therefore unable to get to God, his soul goes to the bottom of a stream, there to remain until, becoming impatient, it demands to be taken out. A ceremony then brings back the tortured soul and makes of it a *"loa nan canarie*—a loa in a jar"*—which thereafter acts as a guard for its family.

There is little agreement as to the place of residence of the loa. In general, it is believed that they come from Guinée each time they are called, returning when they have, in the native idiom, "descended from the heads of their horses"—that is, when the possession of their devotees has ceased. Those "under the water," however, being Haitians, remain in Haiti for seven years until the ceremony just mentioned, of putting them *nan canarie*, has been performed, when they, like the other loa, return to Guinée. At the same time, all recognize

the African character of the loa, whether they be gods brought from
Africa or Créole loa from Haiti itself.

Worship of the loa is directed by priests of the cult. The terms
papaloi and *mamaloi* as designations for male and female priests, almost universally employed by non-Haitian writers, are practically un-
known in Mirebalais, where, as in most regions of Haiti, a priest is
called a *hungan*, a priestess a *mambu*.

An important function of the *hungan* or *mambu* is to foretell the
future, and it is as a diviner that the Vodun priest or priestess is most
often employed. No major rite would be considered by a family unless
divination were resorted to, but consultation is made for a far wider
range of affairs than those of a purely religious nature, and no proposed undertaking of any importance in the secular field is begun
without visiting a diviner to discover whether or not the fates are pro-
pitious. When divining, the priest is usually under possession by his
gods, but other methods, such as gazing into a crystal or basin of
water, may also be employed.

Though a certain hierarchy seems to exist among the *vodun* priests
in other districts of Haiti, in Mirebalais the organization of the cult is
informal to an extreme degree. In the minds of the cult members,
various priests in the same region are differentiated according to the
types of healing in which they have had the greatest success, and the
"miracles" to their credit, such as a *hungan* who had achieved a wide
reputation for being able to resusitate dead children.

Under the hungan and mambu are assistants called *hunsi*, or sometimes, in the case of men, termed *adjanikon*. In some parts of Haiti,
particularly in the plain of the Cul-de-Sac and the Southern penin-
sula, there are degrees of initiation for the hunsi, which include the
ordeal by fire that makes them *hunsi kanzo*. In Mirebalais, however,
the *kanzo* rite, though known by name, is neither required nor
performed. The hunsi and adjanikon know the rituals in a general
way, hold and wave the banners used to salute the gods, sing the songs
for the loa, aid in bringing the possessed dancers out of their possessions, and perform such other ritual tasks as helping the officiating
hungan. Some members of the cult group have special ability to sing
large numbers of the ritual songs for any loa which may be called,

while others perform the animal sacrifices. It is among these male assistants that the most expert drummers are found.

This, then, constitutes an outline of that system of belief included under the term Vodun. Once more, in summary, it may be emphasized that Vodun is neither the practice of black magic, nor the unorganized pathological hysteria it is so often represented to be. The gods are known to their worshippers, and the duties owed them are equally well understood. The reward for the performance of these duties is good health, good harvests, and the goodwill of fellow-men; the punishment for neglect is corresponding ill fortune. On this basis of belief is erected the ceremonial of worship. [See also the section on Religion and Related Aspects of Culture in chapter 3.]

Bibliography

✤ *Following are titles by Melville J. Herskovits that are cited in this volume. For a complete list of Herskovits' works, see Anne Moneypenny and Barrie Thorne, "A Bibliography of the Publications of Melville Jean Herskovits,"* American Anthropologist, 66 (1964):91–109. *Special attention is called to Melville J. Herskovits,* The New World Negro: Selected Papers in Afroamerican Studies (*edited by Frances S. Herskovits*). Bloomington, Indiana: Indiana University Press, 1966; New York: Minerva Press, 1969.

1923 "Some Property Concepts and Marriage Customs of the Vandau." *American Anthropologist* 25:376–86.

1924 "A Preliminary Consideration of the Culture Areas of Africa." *American Anthropologist* 26:50–64.

1926a "Age Changes in Pigmentation of American Negroes." *American Journal of Physical Anthropology* 9:321–27.

1926b "The Cattle Complex in East Africa." *American Anthropologist* 28:230–272; 361–88, 494–528, 633–64.

189

Bibliography

1927a "Acculturation and the American Negro." *Southwestern Political and Social Science Quarterly* 8:211–24.

1927b "Anthropology and Ethnology." *Opportunity* 5:12–13.

1928 *The American Negro: A Study in Racial Crossing.* New York: Alfred A. Knopf, Inc.

1929 "Race Relations in the United States, 1928." *American Journal of Sociology* 34: 1129–39.

1930a "Anthropometry." In *Encyclopedia of the Social Sciences* 2:110–12.

1930b "The Anthropometry of the American Negro." *Columbia University Contributions to Anthropology* 11. New York: Columbia University Press.

1930c "Race Relations, 1929." *American Journal of Sociology* 35:1052–62.

1931 "Domestication." In *Encyclopedia of the Social Sciences* 5:206–08.

1932 Race relations, 1931. *American Journal of Sociology* 36:976–82.

1933 Race relations in 1932. *American Journal of Sociology* 38:913–21.

1934a "Freudian Mechanisms in Negro Psychology." In *Essays Presented to C. G. Seligman,* eds. E. E. Evans-Pritchard, et al. London: Kegan Paul, Trench, Trubner & Co., pp. 75–84. Reprinted in M. J. Herskovits, 1966. *The New World Negro* (q.v.), pp. 135–45.

1934b "Race Mixture." In *Encyclopedia of the Social Sciences* 13:41–43.

1935, 1936 With R. Redfield and R. Linton. "Memorandum for the Study of Acculturation." *Man* 35:145–48; *American Anthropologist* 38:149–52; *American Journal of Sociology* 41:366–70; *Africa* 9:114–18; *Oceania* 6:229–33.

1936a "Applied Anthropology and the American Anthropologists." *Science* 83:215–22.

1936b "The Significance of West Africa for Negro Research." *The Journal of Negro History* 21:15–30.

1937a "African gods and Catholic Saints in New World Negro Belief." *American Anthropologist* 39:635–43.

1937b 'Life in a Haitian Valley.' New York: Alfred A. Knopf, Inc.

1937c "Physical Types of West African Negroes." *Human Biology* 9:483–97.

1937d "The Significance of the Study of Acculturation for Anthropology." *American Anthropologist* 39:259–64.

1938a *Acculturation: The Study of Culture Contact.* New York: J. J. Augustin; reprint ed.: Gloucester, Mass.: Peter Smith, 1958.

1938b *Dahomey: An Ancient African Kingdom.* 2 vols. New York: J. J. Augustin.

1939 *"Some Recent Developments in the Study of West African Native Life."* Journal of Negro History 24:14–32.

Bibliography

1959b "Afro-American Art." *Encyclopedia of World Art* 1:150–58. New York: McGraw-Hill.

1959c "Anthropology and Africa—A Wider Perspective." *Africa* 29:225–38.

1959d "Art and Value." In *Aspects of Primitive Art*, by Robert Redfield, M. J. Herskovits, and G. F. Ekholm, pp. 42–68. New York: The Museum of Primitive Art.

1959e "Past and Present Currents in Ethnology." *American Anthropologist* 61:389–98.

1960a "The Ahistorical Approach to Afro-American Studies: A Critique." *American Anthropologist* 62:559–68.

1960b "United States Foreign Policy; Africa." Hearings before the Committee on Foreign Relations, United States Senate, Eighty-Sixth Congress, Second Session, on March 16, 1960, part I, 105–29. Washington: U.S. Government Printing Office, Sept., 1960.

1962a *The Human Factor in Changing Africa.* New York: Alfred A. Knopf, Inc.

1962b Preface to *Markets in Africa*, eds. Paul Bohannan and George Dalton. Evanston, Ill.: Northwestern University Press.

1964 *Africa and the Problems of Economic Growth.* In *Economic Transition in Africa*, eds., M. J. Herskovits and Mitchell Harwitz. Evanston, Ill.: Northwestern University Press, 3–13.

1966 *The New World Negro*, ed. Frances S. Herskovits. Bloomington: Indiana University Press.

1973 *Cultural Relativism*, ed. F. S. Herskovits. New York: Random House, Vintage Books.

✥ *References to Works in Collaboration with Other Authors*

Herskovits, M. J., Cameron, Vivian K., and Smith, Harriet

1931 "The Physical Form of Mississippi Negroes." *American Journal of Physical Anthropology* 16:193–201.

Herskovits, M. J. and Herskovits, Frances S.

1930 "Bush-Negro Art." *The Arts* 17:25–37,48–49.

1931 "Tales in Pidgin English from Nigeria." *Journal of American Folklore* 44:448–66.

1933 *An Outline of Dahomean Religious Belief.* American Anthropological Association, Memoir 41. Menasha, Wisconsin.

1934a "The Art of Dahomey: I. Brass-Casting and Appliqué Cloths." *The American Magazine of Art* 27:67–76.

1934b "The Art of Dahomey: II. Wood-Carving." *The American Magazine of Art* 27:124–31.

193

Bibliography

1934c *Rebel Destiny; among the Bush Negroes of Dutch Guiana.* New York: Whittlesey House.

1936 *Suriname Folk-Lore.* New York, Columbia University Press.

1938 "Tales in Pidgin English from Ashanti." *Journal of American Folklore* 51:52–101.

1947a "Afro-Bahian Religious Songs: Folk-Music of Brazil." Pamphlet accompanying Album 13, Library of Congress, Recording Laboratory, Music Division, Washington, D.C., 15 pp.

1947b *Trinidad Village.* New York: Alfred A. Knopf, Inc.

1958a *Dahomean Narrative: A Cross-Cultural Analysis.* Evanston, Ill.: Northwestern University Press.

1958b "Sibling Rivalry, the Oedipus Complex, and Myth." *Journal of American Folklore* 71:1–15.

Herskovits, M. J. and Tagbwe, Sie
1930 "Kru Proverbs." *Journal of American Folklore* 43:225–93.

Herskovits, M. J. and Waterman, Richard A.
1949 "Musica de Culto Afrobahiana." *Revista de Estudios Musicales* Año 1, no. 2 (December 1949): 65–127.

✤ References to Works by Other Authors

Abrahams, Roger
1970 "Patterns of Performance in the British West Indies." In *Afro-American Anthropology,* eds. Norman E. Whitten, Jr. (q.v.) and John F. Szwed, pp. 163–79.

Abrahams, Roger D. and Bauman, Richard
1971 "Sense and Nonsense in St. Vincent: Speech Behavior and Decorum in a Caribbean Community." *American Anthropologist* 73:762–72.

American Anthropological Association
1937 "Proceedings of the American Anthropological Association for the Year Ending December 1936." *American Anthropologist* 39:322.

Bascom, William R., and Herskovits, M. J., eds.
1959 *Continuity and Change in African Cultures.* Chicago: University of Chicago Press.

Bastide, Remy
1960 *Les Religions Africaines au Brazil.* Paris: Presses Universitaires de France.

Bennett, Lerone, Jr.
1970 "What's in a Name?" In *Americans from Africa: Old Memories, New Moods,* ed. Peter I. Rose. Chicago: Atherton Press.

Bohannan, Paul
1963 *Social Anthropology.* New York: Holt, Rinehart and Winston.

Bohannan, Paul and Dalton, George, eds.
1962 *Markets in Africa.* Evanston, Illinois: Northwestern University Press.

Bourguignon, Erika
1968 "Trance Dance." *Dance Perspectives* 35:35–36.
1970 "Ritual Dissociation and Possession in Caribbean Negro Religion." *Afro-American Anthropology,* eds. Norman E. Whitten (q.v.) and John F. Szwed, pp. 87–101.

Campbell, Donald T.
1973 Introduction to *Cultural Relativism,* by M. J. Herskovits, v–xiii. (ed. F. S. Herskovits). New York: Random House.

Curtin, Philip D.
1955 *Two Jamaicas; the Role of Ideas in a Tropical Colony, 1830–1865.* Cambridge: Harvard University Press.

Dalton, George
1961 "Economic Theory and Primitive Society." *American Anthropologist* 63:1–25.
1971a *Modernizing Village Economies.* Reading, Mass.: Addison-Wesley Pub. Co.
1971b *Traditional Tribal and Peasant Economies: An Introductory Survey of Economic Anthropology.* Reading, Mass.: Addison-Wesley Pub. Co.

Davenport, F. M.
1905 *Primitive Traits in Religious Revivals.* New York: Macmillan.

Diamond, Stanley
1960 Review of *Continuity and Change in African Culture,* eds. W. R. Bascom and M. J. Herskovits. *American Anthropologist* 62:1085–90.

Dillard, J. E.
1964 "The Writings of Herskovits and the Study of the Language of the Negro in the New World." *Caribbean Studies* 4, no. 2:35–41.

Dorsainvil, J. C.
1931 *Vodou et névrose.* Port-au-Prince: Impr. La Presse.

Dowd, Jerome
1926 *The Negro in American Life.* New York: Century.

Fagg, William
1958 In *The Sculpture of Africa* by E. Elisofon. London: Praeger.

Frazier, E. Franklin
1943 Rejoinder to M. J. Herskovits, "The Negro in Bahia, Brazil: A Problem in Method." *American Sociological Review* 8:403–4.
1949 *The Negro in the United States.* New York: The Macmillan Company.
1957 Introduction to *Caribbean Studies: A Symposium,* ed. Vera Rubin. Kingston, Jamaica: University College of the West Indies.

Freilich, Morris, ed.
1970 *Marginal Natives: Anthropologists At Work.* New York: Harper and Row.

Bibliography

González, Nancie L.
1970 "Toward a Definition of Matrifocality." In *Afro-American Anthropology*, eds. Norman E. Whitten, Jr. (q.v.) and John F. Szwed, pp. 231–44.

Gordon, Milton M.
1964 *Assimilation in American Life*. New York: Oxford.

Greenberg, J. H.
1955 *Studies in African Linguistic Classification*. New Haven: Compass.
1971 "Melville Jean Herskovits." In National Academy of Sciences of the U.S.A., *Biographical Memoirs* 42:66–74. New York: Columbia University Press.

Hammond, Peter B.
1971 *An Introduction to Cultural and Social Anthropology*. New York: Macmillan.

Henney, J. H.
1968 "Spirit Possession Belief and Trance Behavior in a Religious Group in St. Vincent, British West Indies." Ph.D. dissertation, The Ohio State University.

Hoebel, E. A.
1949 Review of *Man and His Works: The Study of Cultural Anthropology*, by M. J. Herskovits. *American Anthropologist* 51:471–74.

Horowitz, Michael M., ed.
1971 *Peoples and Cultures of the Caribbean*. New York: The Natural History Press.

Hsu, Francis, and Merriam, Alan P.
1963 "In Honor of Melville J. Herskovits." *Current Anthropology* 4:92.

Keil, Charles
1966 *Urban Blues*. Chicago: University of Chicago Press.

Kluckhohn, Clyde
1939 "Theoretical Bases for an Empirical Method of Studying the Acquisition of Culture by Individuals." *Man* 39:98–105.

Knight, Frank H.
1952 "Anthropology and Economics." In *Economic Anthropology*, by M. J. Herskovits. New York: Alfred A. Knopf, 508–23. (A critique of *The Economic Life of Primitive Peoples*, by M. J. Herskovits.)

Kreiselman, Mariam
1957 Review of *The Negro family in British Guiana* by R. T. Smith. *American Anthropologist* 59:912–13.

LeClair, Edward E.
1962 "Economic Theory and Anthropology." *American Anthropologist* 64: 1179–1203.

LeClair, Edward E., and Schneider, H. S.
1968   *Economic Anthropology.* New York: Holt, Rinehart, and Winston.

Linton, Adelin and Wagley, Charles
1971   *Ralph Linton.* New York: Columbia University Press.

Linton, Ralph, ed.
1940   *Acculturation in Seven American Indian Tribes.* New York: Appleton-Century.

Lomax, Alan
1970   "The homogeneity of African-Afro-American Musical Style." In *Afro-American Anthropology*, eds. Norman E. Whitten Jr. (q.v.) and John F. Szwed, pp. 181–201.

Merriam, Alan P.
1963   "Melville Jean Herskovits." Booklet prepared for Memorial Service, Northwestern University, March 2, 1963, p. 4.
1964   "Melville Jean Herskovits 1895–1963." *American Anthropologist* 66: 83–91.

Merton, Robert K.
1972   "Insiders and Outsiders: A Chapter in the Sociology of Knowledge." *American Journal of Sociology* 78:9–47.

Messenger, John C., Jr.
1959   "Religious Acculturation among the Anang Ibibio." In *Continuity and Change in African Cultures*, eds. W. R. Bascom and M. J. Herskovits. Chicago: University of Chicago Press, 279–99.

Métraux, Rhoda
1969   Review of *The Influence of Culture on Visual Perception* by Marshall H. Segall, Donald T. Campbell, and M. J. Herskovits. *American Anthropologist* 71:369–71.

Mintz, Sidney W.
1964   "Melville J. Herskovits and *Caribbean Studies:* A Retrospective Tribute." *Carribbean Studies* 4, no. 2:42–51.
1966a   "The Caribbean as a Socio-Cultural area." *Journal of World History* 9:912–37.
1966b   Review of *The Plural Society in the British West Indies* by M. G. Smith. *American Anthropologist* 68:1047.

Mischel, Walter and Frances
1958   "Psychological Aspects of Spirit Possession." *American Anthropologist* 60:249–60.

Moneypenny, Anne, and Thorne, Barrie
1964   "A Bibliography of the Publications of Melville Jean Herskovits." *American Anthropologist* 66:91–109.

Murdock, George P.
1955   Review of *Cultural Anthropology* by M. J. Herskovits. *American Anthropologist* 57:1302–3.

Bibliography

Otterbein, Keith F.
1964   Review of West Indian Family Structure by M. G. Smith. Caribbean Studies 4:74–76.

Pelto, Pertti J.
1970   Anthropological Research: The Structure of Inquiry. New York: Harper & Row.

Polanyi, Karl
1944   The Great Transformation. New York: Rinehart.
1957   "Aristotle discovers the economy." In Trade and Market in the Early Empires, eds. K. Polanyi, C. W. Arensberg, and H. W. Pearson. Glencoe: The Free Press.

Price, Richard
1970   Saramaka Woodcarving: The Development of an Afroamerican Art. Man, n. s. 5:363–78.

Price-Mars, Jean
1928   Ainsi Parla L'Oncle. Paris: Impr. de Compiègne.

Prior, Moody
1963   "Melville Jean Herskovits." Booklet prepared for Memorial Service, Northwestern University, March 2, 1963, p. 5.

Puckett, Newbell N.
1926   Folk Beliefs of the Southern Negro. Chapel Hill: University of North Carolina Press.

Redfield, Robert
1934   "Culture Changes in Yucatan." American Anthropologist 36:57–69. (Quoted in M. J. Herskovits, 1938. Acculturation, 28.)

Redfield, Robert, Ralph Linton, and M. J. Herskovits
1935   "A Memorandum for the Study of Acculturation." Man 35:145–48. American Journal of Sociology 41:366–70. American Anthropologist 38:149–52. Africa 9:114–18. Oceania 6:229–33.

Reisman, Karl
1970   "Cultural and Linguistic Ambiguity in a West Indian Village." In Afro-American Anthropology, eds. Norman E. Whitten, Jr. (q.v.) and John F. Szwed, pp. 129–44.

Ribeiro, René
1949   "The Afrobrazilian Cult-Groups in Recife, Brazil: A Study of Social Adjustment." Master's thesis in Anthropology, Northwestern University.
1960   "An Experimental Approach to the Study of Spirit Possession." Recife, Brazil: Unpublished ms.

Schmidt, Paul
1955   "Some Criticisms of Cultural Relativism." The Journal of Philosophy 52:780–91.

Schneider, Harold K.
1963   Review of *The Human Factor in Changing Africa*, by M. J. Herskovits. *Africa Report* 8:27.

Segall, Marshall H., Campbell, Donald T., and M. J. Herskovits.
1966   *The Influence of Culture on Visual Perception*. Indianapolis: Bobbs-Merrill.

Simpson, George E.
1962   "The Shango Cult in Nigeria and in Trinidad." *American Anthropologist* 64:1204–19.
1968   "Assimilation." *International Encyclopedia of the Social Sciences* 1:438–44. New York: Macmillan.

Simpson, George E. and Hammond, Peter B.
1957   Discussion of "The African Heritage," by M. G. Smith. In *Caribbean Studies: A Symposium*, ed. Vera Rubin, pp. 46–53. Kingston, Jamaica: University College of the West Indies.

Simpson, George E. and Yinger, J. Milton
1972   *Racial and Cultural Minorities*, 4th ed. New York: Harper & Row.

Smith, Michael G.
1957   "The African Heritage in the Caribbean." *In, Caribbean Studies: A Symposium*, ed. Vera Rubin, pp. 34–46. Kingston, Jamaica: University College of the West Indies.
1962   *West Indian Family Structure*. Seattle: University of Washington Press.

Smith, Raymond T.
1956   *The Negro Family in British Guiana*. London: Routledge & Kegan Paul, Ltd.

Social Science Research Council
1954   Summer Seminar on Acculturation. "*Acculturation: An Exploratory Formulation*." *American Anthropologist* 56:973–1002.

Spicer, Edward H.
1968   "Acculturation." In *International Encyclopedia of the Social Sciences* 1:21–26. New York: Macmillan.

Stainbrook, Edward H.
1952   "Some Characteristics of the Psychopathology of Schizophrenic Behavior in Bahian Society." *American Journal of Psychiatry* 109:334 ff.

Taylor, Douglas
1960   "New Languages for Old in the West Indies." *Comparative Studies in Society and History* 3:277–88. (Reprinted in *Peoples and Cultures of the Caribbean*, ed. M. M. Horowitz. New York: The Natural History Press, 1971.)

Bibliography

Vaughan, James H.
1968   "Melville Jean Herskovits." In *International Encyclopedia of the Social Sciences* 6:353–4. New York: Macmillan.

Whiting, John W. M.
1968   "Socialization: Anthropological Aspects." In International Encyclopedia of the Social Sciences 14:545–51. New York: Macmillan.

Whitten, Norman E. Jr., and Szwed, John F., eds.
1970   *Afro-American Anthropology: Contemporary Perspectives.* New York: The Free Press.

Wieschhoff, J. A.
1939   Review of *Dahomey: An Ancient African Kingdom,* by M. J. Herskovits. *American Anthropologist* 41:623.

Wild, Payson
1963   "Melville Jean Herskovits." Booklet prepared for Memorial Service, Northwestern University, March 2, 1963, p. 10.

Wooding, Charles J.
1972   "The Winti-Cult in the Para-District." *Caribbean Studies* 12, no. 1:51–78.

Melville J. Herskovits

GEORGE EATON SIMPSON

Melville Jean Herskovits was the first
Africanist in the United States and the
originator of scientific Afro-American
studies; thus he enjoys the distinction
of having founded two separate
branches of anthropology which are
exerting an increasingly profound
influence on our time. In the present
volume Dr. Simpson provides a fascinating and valuable portrait of
Herskovits the man and the scholar,
plus a group of excerpts from his
writings which will delight the reader
with their lucidity and lively style.

The man: Amiable, witty, and salty-
humored, Melville Herskovits was a
great conversationalist and reveled in
sharp intellectual exchanges, both in
his seminars and among his colleagues.
His wife, Frances, who was a constant
companion on his numerous field trips,
was an important research associate
and coauthor of four books and many
articles. He was a man of seemingly
boundless energy, always an inspira-
tion to his friends and students.

The scholar: A former colleague asserts that Herskovits "knew about all
fields of anthropology as none of us
who came after him do. He was the
last of the all-inclusive anthropologists." In addition to his work on
Africa and Afro-American culture, he
somehow found time to follow his
interests in theoretical anthropology,
art and music, economics, and psychology. These were no mere passing
fancies; Herskovits made fundamental
contributions to each of these anthropological specializations, and was a
pioneer in that area of anthropology
which seeks to apply the discipline's
knowledge to practical affairs. In this
context he was twice called before
Senate committees to give advice on
United States foreign policy in Africa.